ISBN 1-59971-326-8

51200

9 781599 713267

The Fruitful Life: What Will I Be Remembered For?
2nd Edition
Copyright © 2004 by David Drury
Published by Clockwork Publishing
ISBN 1-59971-326-8
www.fruitful-life.com

Printed in the United States of America

Scripture quotations note on page 181 which hereby becomes a part of this copyright page.

Edited by Jean Syswerda
Cover design by Zach Aument
Interior design by Nate Mihalek

Photography
Carl Aurch, Graceline Photography, used by permission
A. Carlos Herrera, used by permission

Dedication

This book is dedicated to the next person you lead into a life-changing relationship with Christ and his church. That person is your fruit in life—and the end goal these chapters have in mind.

May that person see you so connected to the vine that they cannot help but attach themselves to him as well. May you both grow and show fruit together as you follow Christ. And may that person be counted when it counts as your fruit.

Contents

The Fruit of Values

The Fruit of the Disciplines

The Fruit of Multiplication

Introduction:
You're Invited...

You're Invited!

There's nothing quite like hearing those words...

A six-year-old on a boringly muggy day gets a mailed invitation to his best friend's birthday party at the end of June. The licensed characters on the card say, "**You're Invited**" in crayon style first-grader letters. The kid wakes up every day for weeks asking if the party is that day. Swimming pool! Presents! Cake! Ice cream! And he's invited.

A teenager wondering about her popularity at school gets a creative personalized e-mail from the super-popular homecoming queen she barely knows. "**You're Invited!**" It's an after-game party on Friday night and everyone who's anyone will be there. She starts shopping for a new outfit that very afternoon with her mother.

A college girl six months into dating the guy of her dreams gets a phone call from his mother. The mom talks about how serious the two seem to be getting, then mentions the big extended family Christmas gathering they have every year—"**You're Invited!**" Her mind races as she tries not to think too much about what the ring will look like on her hand.

Allison and Trevor decide to go to church for the first time. They don't know anyone. They're nervous about their three kids causing trouble in the service. They nearly leave for embarrassment when one of them makes a funny noise during the prayer. But after the service the couple sitting behind them says "Hi" and strikes up a conversation. When Allison tells them they are new, the nice couple mentions that they love having people over after church each week. "**You're invited today!**" That very hour Allison and Trevor connect with the VanStalk family over a meal. They've been a part of that church for 11 years now.

Red and Joan are empty nesters. Red only sees his neighbors when he mows his lawn. And Joan only sees them when she gets the mail. One day a new couple moves into their cul-de-sac. After getting settled the new couple, Phil & Jennifer, come over to introduce themselves. Before long Phil & Jennifer call them up saying, "**You're invited over for dinner.**" Red and Joan make their first friends in the neighborhood and go to a new small group Phil begins a few months later.

You're Invited...   3

Tim's wife Julia passed away 10 years ago. They would have had their 50th anniversary this coming December. He doesn't believe in going to church and works in the yard on Sundays instead. But several people of all ages in his duplex neighborhood have been nice to him, even though he suspects they're just trying to get him to be religious like they are. They all go to the big church on the corner Tim doesn't care much for. One day in November three of them come over and hand him a big flyer. It says "**You're Invited to Tim & Julia's 50th Anniversary Party.**" He never saw it coming and can't believe they even knew about it. In December his neighbors throw a big bash and get him to pull out his old photos of Julia and remember the best times of his life with her.

You're Invited. You've got to love those words!

YOU'RE INVITED RIGHT NOW

First of all, **you're invited to a party**. One day two thousand years ago Jesus told a story to a gathered crowd about a party that you're already invited to (Matthew 22:1-14; Rev 19:7). The story Jesus told goes like this: There was a king whose son was getting married. He was going to throw a party with a huge banquet that no one would want to miss out on if they knew what it would be like. The king sent out "**You're Invited**" cards to many people in the land. When the wedding banquet was about to begin, he sent out his messengers to remind all the invited people to come to the party. Those he had invited either ignored the reminder because they were too busy or even grabbed the messengers to beat and kill them.

The king retaliated for these slights and crimes and decided that none of the invited guests deserved to come to the huge banquet. The king then told his remaining messengers to "go to the street corners and invite to the banquet anyone you find." Jesus said that the messengers gathered all kinds of people who were willing to come to the party—good people and bad people—and the wedding hall was packed.

This is the party that you are invited to. You already have an invitation. If you have forgotten what it's all about then this is your reminder. Jesus is the King's son, and he wants you at the party. You just have to get ready and show up for the festivities. If you haven't accepted this part of the invitation, I'd like you to spend this week thinking about it, then decide whether or not you'd like to get ready for the party in heaven.

There's more to the invitation. You can invite all your friends! Think of it as an e-mail that you can easily forward on to other people in your contact list. Or like a big stack of invitations to the party that were sent to you with the postage already paid. You've just got to mail them out to people you know.

This second part of the invitation means telling others, **"You're invited too."** Most of us instinctively know that we should increase our efforts to get more people, good and bad, to that party in heaven. The problem is we're frustrated with the results. Much we've tried hasn't seemed to work. Other ideas seem way too difficult and strange. We see so much risk and failure in inviting others to Jesus' party—and so we start to think the professional messengers should just do it instead of us. You know who the professional messengers are: the pastors and the priests and the missionaries. But we sense that is not the way the King wants it. We sense that we're supposed to be messengers, too. We wonder if some of the people we know, good and bad, won't be at the party in heaven.

Which is the reason for the third part of this invitation. You're invited to get the most of this book by fully engaging with it. If you do you can radically change the number of people at that party because of your life. Here are some real life ways to begin to fully engage in The Fruitful Life:

• Participate in the *40 Days: The Fruitful Life* with the whole church. When a crowd of people get pumped up about something God is doing in all of them at the same time, something special happens. Prayer and fasting as a larger community will help to deepen the impact.

• *Meet for six straight weeks with a small group* and discuss these issues in your own way. This could be your current small group, a Bible study, a class, an accountability group or even just a group of 3-12 friends (good or bad) or 3-6 couples. Write the names of those you can do this with here:

• *Read one chapter a day*. If you don't already have a set time each day to pause to pray, read or journal, this is the time to start. Your group will be a great encouragement in this. There are 40 chapters here. If you get behind, catch up right away to experience the same concepts with others at the same time. If you finish a chapter early, don't read ahead. Just look more deeply into the Bible passages mentioned, journal or re-read that day's chapter. Check out the suggested resources listed with some chapters. Again, experience this with others at the same pace and it will deepen the impact.

Are you ready to accept the invitation? To get ready for the party? Then let's do it together. For the next 40 days let's take a look at what the Bible says about fruit in our lives.

Happy are those who do not follow the advice of the wicked,
or take the path that sinners tread,
or sit in the seat of scoffers

But their delight is in the law of the Lord,
and on his law they meditate day and night.

They are like trees planted by streams of water,
which yield their fruit in its season,
and their leaves do not wither.
In all that they do, they prosper.

Psalm 1:1-3 (NRSV[1])

the fruit of the vine

Fruit is not optional. Healthy things grow and produce. It is as natural for a Jesus-follower as it is in nature. Unfortunately, believers often struggle to produce fruit. They don't reach out to unbelievers as they know they should. They lack fruit.

By considering what Jesus said in John 15 you can re-imagine evangelism in terms of your own connection to God. Instead of just "doing" evangelism, you'll learn to make the fruitful life a part of who you are all the time.

Week One Memory Verse:

I am the vine; you are the branches.
If a man remains in me and I in him, he will bear much fruit;
apart from me you can do nothing.
– John 15:5

Getting Connected to Christ

It's all about your connection to Christ.

At the end of your life, the most important thing for which you will be remembered is how connected you were to Jesus Christ. The legacy you leave behind on planet earth will be a direct result of the quality of this connection in your life. Nothing of lasting value happens outside of Christ. Notice the word, "lasting" there. That's the operative term.

LASTING VALUES AND LAWN MOWING VALUES

There are so many valuable ways to spend your time. I mow my grass most Saturdays. It's a valuable use of my time. The Saturdays I skip mowing the lawn reinforce this value. When it grows so tall that the neighborhood kids play hide and go seek in the thick stuff, I am reminded that mowing the lawn is an important thing to do. My value for lawn mowing increases. So I do it. It has some value in life. However, mowing my lawn doesn't have lasting value. There's nothing eternal about it.

Eternal values are the things that last. The ones that really matter after your time on earth is done. And these lasting values flow directly from Christ. I can't do much of lasting value on my own. But the Bible tells me I can do all things through Christ who gives me strength (Philippians 4:13). It's my connection to Jesus that enables, empowers and energizes me to do things of lasting value. No other connection counts like this connection. I know some people who are pretty well connected. In fact, a few of them are what you would call "name-droppers." These are the people who continually work into conversations what famous person they happened to be talking to earlier. They try to make these name-dropping times very casual, "Oh, the other day I was talking to so-and-so-famous-person and they said…" Sometimes I like to mess with these people and say to them, "You know, the other day the Pope, Bono, the President and I were having coffee, and they said…"

WHO YOU KNOW

But having connections really does help in life. Who you know is so important in finding work and getting what you want that you are naturally envious of people with better connections, and you work hard to develop better connections yourself. I feel this way myself sometimes. I wonder, "If I only knew that person or more people in that field, then I could really accomplish something." The problem is that all these connections count for nothing when it comes to eternity.

When the end of your life arrives, the most important thing will not be how well you knew your pastor, how much you know about Bible stories, or what important Christian person was your friend. When the end comes, it's all about your connection to Christ. He's the only name you can drop to get into heaven.

OUR CONNECTION TO "THE LEAST"

Jesus told another story about that last moment in our lives, and it is recorded for us in Matthew 25:31-46. In this story Jesus tells us that one day he will sit on his throne in heaven and divide all the people who ever lived into two groups. Jesus calls one of these groups "goats" and the other "sheep." Now, there's a tough choice. Personally, I wouldn't like to be either a sheep or a goat. But that's what Jesus calls them. Then Jesus will tell the sheep on his right, "Come, you who are blessed by my Father; take your inheritance, the kingdom prepared for you since the creation of the world. For I was hungry and you gave me something to eat, I was thirsty and you gave me something to drink, I was a stranger and you invited me in, I needed clothes and you clothed me, I was sick and you looked after me, I was in prison and you came to visit me."

What Jesus Cares about is that we are connected to him with the kind of intensity that shows in the way we live our lives.

Well, this comes as quite a shock to the "sheep," Jesus tells us. They don't recall ever doing any of those things to Jesus. So as a group they ask Jesus, when did we do any of those things to you?

Jesus answers, "I tell you the truth, whatever you did for one of the least of these brothers of mine, you did for me." Jesus makes it clear that when these "sheep" met people's needs—even strangers—here on earth they were in effect doing it for him! And so those on his right get to spend eternity with him. His presence in their lives produced fruit—so he gives them their reward.

The Fruit of the Vine   Day 01   9

Then Jesus turns to those on his left, the "goats." Now, you have to wonder why this group doesn't see it coming. They just watched all the sheep get the prize, and they're in the "other group," and Jesus is calling them "goats" and all. Jesus says to them, "Depart from me, you who are cursed, into the eternal fire prepared for the devil and his angels. For I was hungry and you gave me nothing to eat, I was thirsty and you gave me nothing to drink, I was a stranger and you did not invite me in, I needed clothes and you did not clothe me, I was sick and in prison and you did not look after me."

The "goats" are in shock! They don't recall ever having the opportunity to help Jesus out of these problems. They would remember something like that. If Jesus called me up on the phone and said, "Hey, I'm sick and in prison and I could use a good meal and something to quench my thirst. Could you stop by, and bring me a change of clothes—I don't have any." I would remember that! The "goats" protest and as a group ask Jesus, when did we not do those things to help you?

Jesus answers, "I tell you the truth, whatever you did not do for one of the least of these, you did not do for me."

FRUIT THAT LASTS

This is a hard thing for us to hear. If we're honest, most of us admit we don't do these things for others much at all. Our shortcomings make us feel guilty—so we choose to ignore them. We move on to other religious activities that fill the void. We choose the Christian fruit that we can manage more easily: going to church, acting like polite Christians, not sinning in public, displaying Christian items in our homes or workplaces or vehicles. These "evidences" of being a "sheep" are more manageable to us. They help us "feel" like we have Christian fruit in our lives.

It's fruit that lasts.

But Jesus didn't ask the goats what kind of bumper stickers they had. He asked what things of lasting value they had done. He was only concerned about eternal fruit.

These other evidences of our connection to Christ aren't wrong—it's just that they aren't eternal. What Jesus wants is for us to be connected to him with the kind of intensity that lights up the way we live our lives. That's what eternal fruit is all about. It's fruit that lasts!

Day 02

Spiritual Formation for Ordinary People

Don't worry…you can do it!

That first chapter may have bothered you a bit… poured a little more guilt on your already burdened back. You might be wondering, "I don't need even more of this guilt in my life." You're right. But a reminder of what's important in life never hurt anyone. Jesus told that story so you'd be sure to know what counts most to him.

But how do you get there?

That's the key question. How do ordinary people get connected to Christ in such a way that lasting fruit is a constant part of their lives? This question alone is a good reason for the church to exist. For two-thousand years followers of Jesus Christ have gathered together and asked versions of this question and worked on ways to make it happen.

So, if we study the history of great Christians and Christian movements—how they lived and how they produced fruit that lasted—we actually find some answers to our question:

HOW DO ORDINARY PEOPLE GET CONNECTED TO CHRIST AND SHOW LASTING FRUIT?

Ordinary people become so intensely connected to Christ that in all they do they show the fruit of that connection.

But in order to get that connected to Christ…

Ordinary people first need to experience long phases of growth in their connection so that their power in life truly comes from Christ. Paul talked of this when he wrote to the Galatian church he had started. He said, "But oh, my dear children! I feel as if I am going through labor pains for you again, and they will continue until Christ is fully developed in your lives" (Galatians 4:19 NLT). Other versions say "fully formed in you." Eugene Peterson paraphrased it as "until Christ's life becomes visible in your lives…"[2] Pastor Paul looked at his people and compared these long phases of growth to the pains of childbirth! This is what spiritual formation is all about: a long—and sometimes painful—process of growth.

But in order to grow in this connection…

Ordinary people first need to leave behind anything that hinders them in their relationship with Christ. The book of Hebrews speaks to this directly when it says, "Therefore, since we are surrounded by such a huge crowd of witnesses to the life of faith, let us strip off every weight that slows us down, especially the sin that so easily hinders our progress. And let us run with endurance the race that God has set before us. We do this by keeping our eyes on Jesus, on whom our faith depends from start to finish" (Hebrews 12:1-2a NLT). There are things in life that weigh us down and entangle us. These "things" are often sins we must confess and root out. Other things that hinder us in the race? Reliance on our own strength. Relying on anything but Christ for our salvation. Anything that entangles us and restricts our freedom in Christ. These things must be rooted out by believing the truth of Scripture about our own identity.

Ordinary people become so intensely connected to Christ that in all they do they show the fruit of that connection.

But in order to leave these things behind…

Ordinary people first need to cross the line and commit to Jesus Christ as their Savior. I know the very day that I "became a Christian" back in 1980. It was July 21st in College Wesleyan Church. It gives me great assurance to look back at that day and know I "crossed the line of faith." However, times are changing and people are coming to Christ in a longer process of salvation. People have a harder time pinpointing one day or month where they "crossed the line of faith." The church has adapted to this change and no longer calls people to "come to the altar" or "raise your hand" to say you're accepting Christ. Often the call to commit is very private. These changes may be needed, but at the same time we still need to know, really know, that we've crossed the line.

Going Deeper

If you are seeking freedom in Christ from anything that "entangles" you and is holding back your spiritual formation in Christ I suggest that you read Neil Anderson's book

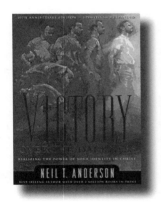

Victory Over the Darkness: Realizing the Power of Your Identity in Christ. Ventura, CA: Gospel Light © 2000.

Two great ways to still have this assurance even if you don't know the exact date when you committed your life to Christ are baptism and communion. These two oldest of Christian practices offer a great way for you to be assured that you've "crossed the line." By being baptized, you're physically showing that you've crossed the line and are ready to begin the process of leaving behind the things that "hinder." Baptism is a great line to cross. And the Lord's Supper is another great line to cross. By taking communion in church, you are saying "I am a part of Christ, and he is a part of me." If you can say that—perhaps for the first time—then make the Lord's Supper your line to cross.

But in order to cross that line and commit…

Ordinary people first have to come to grips with their sin. Realizing that we have all sinned is the key, confessing that opens the lock, and asking for forgiveness of that sin pushes the door wide open. Realizing that all have sinned is as simple as this verse: "For all have sinned, and come short of the glory of God" (Romans 3:23 KJV). Confessing and asking for forgiveness is as simple as this one: "If we confess our sins he is faithful and just to forgive us our sins and cleanse us from all unrighteousness" (1 John 1:9). These two oft-quoted verses are where every seeker starts on the journey.

But in order to come to grips with their sin…

Ordinary people first need to be walked through all the above by someone who loves them. We often call this evangelism. We also call it discipleship. Both words sound scary and intimidating to many. But in the end they both have the same starting point and ending point, so it's kind of hard to distinguish between the two. Jesus told us to go and make disciples and that seems to imply both ideas in one. So let's begin to think that way again. Don't be someone "into" evangelism.

How beautiful are the feet of those who bring good news!

Don't be "more of a discipleship person than an evangelist." Jesus didn't draw a line between the two, so we shouldn't. We should focus on walking with other ordinary people through this whole process, from beginning to end. And walking them through it takes more than five minutes. It may take five months or five years. With some, it may even take five decades. But walk with them. You may get stuck with someone at the second phase or third for years. Don't give up on them. Keep walking with them.

Romans 10:14-15 says, "How, then, can they call on the one they have not believed in? And how can they believe in the one of whom they have not heard? And how can they hear without someone preaching it to them? And how can they preach unless they are sent? As it is written, 'How beautiful are the feet of those who bring good news!'" So, it's all up to you and your beautiful feet! No pressure! Just keep walking.

What Does It Mean To Abide?

You're just a branch.

Many Christians today talk about their "relationship" with Jesus Christ. Maybe that completely makes sense to you. But you might be like a lot of the rest of ordinary people trying to figure out just how we have a "relationship" with this man who lived 2,000 years ago, who also is the Son of the Most High God. If you're in the latter group and are still looking for ways to make sense of what this relationship looks like, then this is the chapter for you.

One day Jesus sat down with his disciples and explained what this relationship is supposed to look like. In John 15 he briefly shares one of the most beautiful word pictures ever conceived. What he shares is the absolute core of what it means to have a relationship with him. And what he shares is the absolute key to The Fruitful Life.

Take the time right now to read what he said:

"I am the true vine, and my Father is the gardener. He cuts off every branch in me that bears no fruit, while every branch that does bear fruit he prunes so that it will be even more fruitful. You are already clean because of the word I have spoken to you. Remain in me, and I will remain in you. No branch can bear fruit by itself; it must remain in the vine. Neither can you bear fruit unless you remain in me.

"I am the vine; you are the branches. If a man remains in me and I in him, he will bear much fruit; apart from me you can do nothing. If anyone does not remain in me, he is like a branch that is thrown away and withers; such branches are picked up, thrown into the fire and burned. If you remain in me and my words remain in you, ask whatever you wish, and it will be given you. This is to my Father's glory, that you bear much fruit, showing yourselves to be my disciples.

"As the Father has loved me, so have I loved you. Now remain in my love. If you obey my commands, you will remain in my love, just as I have obeyed my Father's commands and remain in his love. I have told you this so that my joy may be in you and that your joy may be complete. My command is this: Love each other as I have loved you. Greater love has no one than this, that he lay down his life for his friends. You are my friends if you do what I command. I no longer call you servants, because a servant does not know his master's business. Instead, I have called you friends, for everything that I learned from my Father I have made known to you. You did not choose me, but I chose you and appointed you to go and bear fruit—fruit that will last. Then the Father will give you whatever you ask in my name. This is my command: Love each other."

Wow! It's going to take us at least another 37 days to truly comprehend the meaning of what Jesus says here. Isn't that always the way Jesus works? He says just a little bit and then we're caught thinking it through for so long afterwards. The original 12 disciples felt this way all the time—so we're not in bad company. We'll just do what they did: ask a lot of questions and be patient with God and ourselves as we live out the answers.

THE KEY NOUN: VINEYARD

The first big question we have has to do with the noun. By noun I'm speaking of the whole word picture itself. How do vines, branches and gardeners work anyway? Most of us don't have vineyards growing in our backyards so we need to know a bit more.

Vines are plants that twist and turn as they grow. They can become almost tree-like in their quality, with branches that bear fruit. They grow along the ground, up a fence or vine-post, or even up a building or another tree.

The key concept for Christ is the fruit that the branches of a vine produce. They produce grapes…but for Jesus these grapes had a profound meaning. What does Jesus mean when he talks of "fruit" to his disciples?

Fruit is a matter of qualities and results. Fruit can either be a quality that is grown in you because of your healthy connection to the vine of Jesus Christ. Or it can be results that are grown from you because of that same healthy connection. The entire key to The Fruitful Life is ensuring you are connected to Christ in such a way that you have these qualities and results in your life.

The key to The Fruitful Life is ensuring you are connected to Christ in such a way that you have these qualities and results in your life.

The Fruitful Life

THE KEY VERB: ABIDING

The second big question has to do with the verb. By verb I'm speaking of the word "remain." What does Jesus mean by that? In some translations we have the word "abide" instead. Jesus says it over and over in this talk with his disciples. It's the key verb of the entire conversation. It all hinges on "remaining" or rather, "abiding." We should figure that out.

What is abiding?

ABIDING IS A MATTER OF LOCATION

Abiding in the Bible is used to mean "not to stray." This has the connotation of location. Abiding is about where you are. Whenever the Bible talks about being "in Christ" or "in God" (and it does so very often), it has this meaning of abiding. Are you remaining in him? That's the key question for the man or woman who wants a fruitful life. Saint Augustine, when distributing the elements at the Eucharist, would say to his parishioners, "receive what you already are; become what you receive." By being in Christ your identity is wrapped up in who he is. Your location is entirely in him.

> *"Receive what you already are; become what you receive."*
> *-- Saint Augustine*

ABIDING IS A MATTER OF DURATION

Abiding in the Bible is also meant to point to duration. Abiding in the location mentioned (namely, Jesus Christ), continually or for a length of time. When Paul tells you to "pray continually," (1 Thessalonians 5:17), it is another instruction related to abiding.

ABIDING IS A MATTER OF OBEDIENCE

As is clearly stated in John 15, abiding is also a simple matter of obedience. The branch does what the vine tells it to do. The church is often called the body of Christ. And likewise many often refer to Christ as the head. Well, your body, except for some major injury to your nervous system, does what the head tells it to do. If you want your left hand to grab the toothpaste and your right the toothbrush, they do these things. That is the intended way for the church to react to Christ. When it's not happening, that's disobedience. And that means a major injury to your spiritual nervous system must be breaking down your communication and connection to Christ.

ABIDING IS A MATTER OF ENDURANCE

But abiding is not only about where and how long and what you do for Christ. It also means enduring whatever may try to cut it off—hardship, tragedy, suffering or hurtful times. Abiding means finishing well—not just starting off great. It means you abide—you stay connected to the vine—during the joyful journey as well as when you walk through the valley of the shadow of death. When you pull through something with Christ you are abiding.

ABIDING IS A MATTER OF UNITY

By unity I mean that we are united in Christ in such a way that we're nearly indistinguishable from him. We are connected with Christ in a unique and preferable way. There is almost a sense of equality in the words Jesus uses in John 15:15. He says, "I no longer call you servants…Instead I have called you friends, for everything that I learned from my Father I have made known to you." It is as though Christ elevates us to achieve what he achieved and use the power he has. As Martin Luther said, "All that Christ has now becomes the property of the believing soul; all that the soul has, becomes the property of Christ."

But you're still just a branch. Don't confuse your role. When Jesus speaks to you in John, you see that you're just a branch attached to him and that your identity in that role is the key to your fruitfulness. When you abide in the location that is Christ, and do so for a long duration out of obedience and with endurance, you receive the benefits of unity in Christ. You become fruitful, because that which is attached to the vine bears fruit. It's just how it works.

Rechargeable Batteries or Extension Cords?

Your power comes from your connection.

You are powerless on your own. All of your frustrations in life come from trying to take control over things you have no power to control. And what has drawn you closer to God than anything was getting to the place where you admitted this powerlessness and went to him to get through. This is why the biggest crises of your life have made you think the most about God. This is contrary to human logic. You would think that tough times would make you run from God. Yes, sometimes people use the worst things in their lives to shut out God and the world—but over time, or many times in the privacy of their own minds, they are asking God for help.

But even after you've admitted your powerlessness over things you can't control, you can drift into depending on yourself and others for strength. You forget that your power comes from your connection to Christ.

TWO POWER DRILLS

I like tools. I'm a man, so that is nearly mandatory. I especially like drills. Drills are very manly. They're like hammers in their manliness. Except they are even better, because they also include a little thing called "power." When holding a power drill I can see myself taking apart or putting together anything in my entire house. I've found the first task to be easier than the second…but anyway, that's how it makes me feel.

For years I had this wimpy little power drill with a rechargeable battery. The bottom of the drill would slide out and I would put it in a plug-in station where it would charge up after it ran out of "juice" (as I always call it). That was the theory, at least. It had two problems, however. First, I would always forget to recharge the battery when I was done with a big job. After I was done doing some incredibly manly project for my wife, I would toss the drill in my pile of tools and go watch football. I would forget to recharge. Then when I wanted to use it again for even a simple little screw-turning job, it would make that depressing winding down noise and I would have to complain to my wife about not getting the job done. Secondly, the drill also had a "memory problem." You may know what I'm talking about here if you own an older digital camera or video camera, or, if you happen to have had this same drill I had. Some rechargeable batteries have a "memory," I'm told. They tell me (and by "they" I mean, "men more manly than me") that these batteries remember at what point they were recharged the last time. So if I had 75% of my power used up when I recharged the battery, then the next time I used it the battery would begin to shut down with 25% of its "juice" still left. Not having enough man-smarts to understand this, nor the patience to stand for 30 minutes running out the last bit of juice, I would recharge the battery before all its juice was out. So, after several years using my wimpy powerless drill, it would max out when recharging with only about 3% of its power potential. I could lock the gears and then manually turn the whole drill around in circles to drill in a screw, but that's about all it was good for—a very heavy, awkward and elaborate screw driver.

During these days of powerless drill problems, I would reminisce of the days when I was a little boy and my father would go into the garage to get his power drill. He would come back with a little case of drill bits and the most massive and simple drill in the world. It was mostly the color of plain silver steel, as though any decorations or color would have offended its manly manufacturer. It had only one button, which was the trigger. No adjustments needed. It had one speed: "Super-Manly Speed." All it could do was drill a hole to China. I loved that drill. I would have traded a thousand of my wimpy powerless drills for that baby! There was one main difference between Dad's drill and mine.

His drew its power through an extension cord. Sure—he lost a bit of independence because of that. He couldn't go out into a field far away from the house and drill things. But since 99% of the time we were in the garage or the house with outlets everywhere, that didn't matter. His drill—decades older than mine—worked so well because it was directly connected to the source of power!

Are you?

Christian culture today has become largely rechargeable. We ask people to stop in from time to time to the church building and get their spiritual batteries recharged. We file in, hook up, charge up, and then head out. We're independent. We think this system makes us more versatile, more able to take our faith wherever we want. But too often we forget to recharge. We feel worn out in nearly every way. Our spiritual recharge memory lets so much go in one ear and out the other. We don't "get as much out of" church as we used to. We don't feel fed enough. So early in the week we hear our spiritual battery making that depressing winding down sound.

We need to get back to the extension cord method as Christians. We need to be directly connected to the source of power! We may feel like we lose a bit of independence by being so 100% dependent on Christ, but we won't miss it. Our independence is only giving us headaches. We need a simple and full-time connection to Christ. Then when we go to our churches, it's not to "get something out of it"… it's to "give something to it." And when we reach out to those around us, we won't be caught winding down on our own batteries. Instead, we'll transfer the power of Christ directly to them from the source.

Now that sounds pretty manly to me!

We need to be directly connected to the source of power!

Day 05

Spiritual Pruning

Sometimes you just need an extreme spiritual makeover.

Did you ever look in the mirror and not like what you saw? During some seasons of life we actually avoid mirrors. Or other times we move into obsessive-compulsive mirror-gazing. We look to change every little problem we see in ourselves. Nearly all junior-high kids come to a point when they don't like what they see—and unfortunately, our bodies are not usually too kind to us when we reach the very age when we start to care about the way we look.

MAKEOVER MODE

In order to solve this mirror problem, people go into "makeover mode." The way people react to this amazes me to this day—even though it's commonplace in our culture. A young woman's friends will surprise her by showing up with video cameras and TV producers who spring the "good" news on her: we're going to give you a makeover. Now, every time I've ever seen this happen, the girl getting the makeover is ecstatic with joy on camera. Yes! I'm getting made over! But what I don't get is why that person isn't totally offended. Her friends are basically saying, "You look bad. So bad in fact that you will need professionals to improve your looks." They don't pull her aside and tell her this confidentially, which would be bad enough in my mind. Instead, they spring it on her while being filmed for our enjoyment and her embarrassment. Sometimes they do this on live TV! I just don't get it.

There must be something in those makeover target women that is so strong that it overcomes the embarrassment. Some urge so intense that they respond with joy when told they look bad. That urge must be the desire to change. The desire to be different than they already are. The desire to be better than they have been. We all have this in us. We want to change. But how?

SPIRITUAL

We get this urge when we examine our spiritual selves as much as our physical selves. Every once in a while we take a too long, too hard look at our spiritual lives. We see every tiny blemish and ugly wrinkle in our spiritual faces. Most days we try to cover these up with our cheerful responses to "how ya doin?" We even pretend to be mostly content with our spiritual growth when asked or when thinking about it. We reason, "I'm doing better than most." But from time to time, the spiritual makeup comes off, and we take a good long look at who we really are. At that point, we usually feel two things: a deep sense of guilt and a desire to change.

THE RIGHT KIND OF GUILT

The first kind of guilt is primary guilt. This is the gnawing kind of guilt that gets at us from the inside. Usually we feel disappointed with ourselves when experiencing this kind of guilt. We get down on ourselves. Every once in a while when I'm driving in a car with my wife or even just sitting in the living room, I will make a noticeable grunt or low sigh. My wife will say, "What's wrong?" This kicks me out of my thought pattern. Nearly every time that happens, I realize that I am getting down on myself about something. I feel guilty about something I did wrong. It is primary guilt. And the guilt I feel may be 10 days or 10 years old! That inner primary guilt can paralyze me and make me lose all sense of identity as a Christian. Romans 8:2 says, "Because through Christ Jesus the law of the Spirit of life set me free from the law of sin and death." I need to remember that Christ has set me free from primary guilt—and through him I can live in the Spirit.

We all have this in us. We want to change. But how?

Guilt is often a negative motivator. Many feelings of guilt come from other people. That's the second kind of guilt. It's called secondary guilt. This secondary guilt is unhelpful and may weigh us down and even incapacitate us. Guilt is "heaped on" us by others. You can be freed from that kind of guilt. "There is now no condemnation for those who are in Christ Jesus." (Romans 8:1). Guilt heaped on us is condemnation. Others condemn us and give us the ugly gift of secondary guilt. That's a gift we should not accept. Return to sender.

The third kind of guilt is altogether different. It is spiritual guilt. Spiritual guilt is hard to discern from the other two kinds of guilt. Often we will feel guilty about our spiritual lives, but it might not actually be spiritual guilt. It is quite possible to feel guilty about not doing this or that spiritual task or discipline, but only because someone else is heaping that guilt on us. That is just secondary guilt applied to spiritual things. We also get down on our-selves about our progress spiritually. We look in the spiritual mirror and don't like what we see—this is often just primary guilt applied to spiritual things. We must realize that spiritual guilt doesn't come from ourselves or from others. It comes from the Spirit of God. Spiritual guilt is not negative, but positive. The Spirit points out what is in need of true change and immediately offers the solution to overcoming it. There is a sure-fire way to tell whether the guilt you are experiencing is true spiritual guilt or one of the other kinds of guilt. If there just seems to be no forgiveness or way out of that guilt, then it was likely heaped on you by others or boiled up in you as primary guilt. If you feel that forgiveness is possible and there is a way to overcome the guilt, then it is most likely being offered by the Spirit. In Hebrews 10:22 it says, "Let us draw near to God with a sincere heart in full assurance of faith, hav-ing our hearts sprinkled to cleanse us from a guilty conscience." When you feel that sense of spiritual guilt, draw near to God and be assured that his forgiveness and way out cleanses you completely.

The process just described is grace. God never gives guilt without grace. There's a les-son here to learn and live. Never accept guilt that isn't accompanied by freeing grace. This is true for yourself and the way you view others. If you find guilt in yourself, allow grace within you to overcome it. If you find guilt in others, allow grace toward them to overshadow it! The guilt is there—it's a matter of fact and a fact of life. But the grace of God is powerful against it.

THE RIGHT KIND OF CHANGE

The second thing we often feel when looking in the spiritual mirror is the desire to change. We feel spiritual guilt and know we need to live differently. We know we want to be better than we've been.

But often we try to change on our own. We use methods that others suggest. We mimic them. It often doesn't work. We don't change in the end. We're the same. We're often even worse, because we lose our motivation to change since we tried and failed.

This is all because we're trying to change ourselves. It just doesn't work. Men and women have been trying to change themselves for thousands of years. Take a look around. Pretty obvious that it hasn't worked, isn't it? We need an outside source for change.

In John 15:1-2 Jesus gives us the key to change. Continuing with his beautiful imagery about the vine and branches, he says, "My Father is the gardener. He cuts off every branch in me that bears no fruit, while every branch that does bear fruit he prunes so that it will be even more fruitful." In the first part here, we see the stark reality that fruit is expected and required. In the second part of that verse we read about the spiritual pruning process God works in us. For those branches that show some fruit—God takes a specific action. He doesn't just slap us on the back and say, "Way to go!" and move on. No, he pulls out his knife and cuts us!

"My Father is the gardener. He cuts off every branch in me that bears no fruit." – John 15:1

Okay, now it does not seem that positive at this point, does it? I heard one guy interpreting this passage, and he said, "I've read John 15 and the way I see it, I'm gonna get cut either way so I better give up." That's not Jesus' intention at all here. Pruning is the process of cutting away the excess on a branch to focus the energy on new growth. If we don't allow God to prune us in this way, then we won't change. In Matthew 5:29 during his Sermon on the Mount, Jesus says, "If your right eye causes you to sin, gouge it out and throw it away. It is better for you to lose one part of your body than for your whole body to be thrown into hell." Now that's an extreme makeover! Why does Jesus say these extreme things? Because we need to wake up to the reality that fruit is what counts and the things that cause us to sin hold back the production of fruit.

GOING UNDER THE KNIFE

Those in "makeover mode" will sometimes go to such extremes as getting plastic or recon- structive surgery. Some shows on television document this self-obsessive and emotionally tormenting process. They often call it "going under the knife" to improve themselves.

Wouldn't it make more sense to go under God's pruning knife instead? That's his perfect plan for us. In a world obsessed with changing everything about our outsides, we've so often failed to let God change a thing about our insides. Hebrews 12:1 says, "Let us throw off everything that hinders and the sin that so easily entangles." We branches could bear so much more fruit if we allowed God to do this pruning work in us. We can't do this surgery on ourselves. Those who have tried know the scars it leaves. How much better—and more effective—to let the Great Physician cut out what he knows we don't need anymore, to prune off anything that hinders a fruitful life.

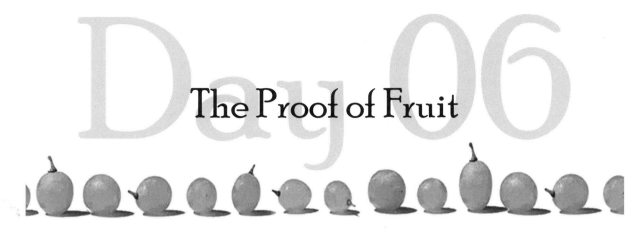

The Proof of Fruit

Fruit is natural for every believer.

If you have a plant in your garden or landscaping around your house, you expect it to grow and be healthy. If all the conditions are right, it will. If that plant doesn't grow and doesn't produce fruit in the proper season, then there is a problem. Not enough sun, or too much? Not enough water, or again, too much? More fertilizer perhaps? Maybe a rodent is chewing on it?

Whatever the case, if your plant isn't producing, you go hunting for the reasons and solutions. But, two things you don't do: You don't simply assume it's a bad plant—as though it wasn't made right. You also don't start expecting less of the plant—as though it wasn't meant to grow and produce.

> *Fruit is natural for every believer.*

You were meant to grow and produce. And you were made just right for the job.

The church has become too complacent with lack of fruit. When a plant doesn't grow and produce, we try to figure out why. We look to change the conditions so fruit becomes a possibility. So, when a disciple doesn't grow and produce, why do we go hunting for excuses and justifications? Why do we assume we just weren't made to produce like other people? Why do we start expecting less of ourselves—as though we weren't meant to grow and produce?

Here's why…

WE VALUE CONDITIONS MORE THAN THE FRUIT

The church today is too often conditions-centered rather than fruit-focused. After centuries of Christianity, some patterns emerged about what spiritual conditions produced the most fruit in the lives of ordinary disciples: prayer, going to church, devotional reading of Scripture, giving, doing good deeds, meeting the needs of the down-and-out, being nice to each other, singing songs to God, proclaiming the Gospel to others, and fasting. These and other conditions over time have shown themselves to be key ingredients in the lives of fruit-producing disciples. So in a logical way when fruit was absent, adding a little more of one of these spiritual conditions should make a disciple grow and produce more fruit.

This made sense. However, over time the focus shifted from noticing fruit to noticing the conditions that usually caused it. This conditions-centered Christianity accelerated through the church's history. The problem is that any discerning believer from the Apostle Paul to my grandmother can tell you that you can do the things on that list and still not have your heart in the right place. You can do the actions and create the conditions and still not be truly connected to Christ. You can center your life on conditions and still not produce fruit.

The fruit comes from your connection to Christ. And you cannot grow outside of him.

Even worse, Christians have gone from focusing their Christian walk on the conditions that produce fruit to focusing just on certain *ways* to practice the conditions. The way we do certain things has become even more important than what we're doing as Christians. We mimic the spiritual habits of other Christians and assume they will produce fruit. But somewhere along the way we forgot the point—not to look and act like other Christians but to produce fruit! The conditions and actions that produce fruit in one Christian's life may not actually work in another's.

WE ENJOY PROOF THAT WE CAN CREATE ON OUR OWN

One time my wife bought a present for my grandmother when we were visiting her in Arizona. She bought a box of those ornately carved soaps that some people display in their bathrooms. Being an uncultured man, I've never understood those soaps. They're just for looks, my wife tells me. Why they're made of soap, then, I don't know.

Once we got back home we got word that Grandma had opened the box and didn't realize they were soaps. She thought they were chocolates. After a big soapy bite, she realized her mistake.

When it comes to our spiritual lives, the proof is in the fruit. It's required. Fruit is not optional.

Some things appear to be one thing but are actually another. We human beings are great at making something look like something else. The only thing we do better than imitation is manipulation. We manipulate people into thinking something is what it isn't. Entire industries such as advertising and public relations are caught up in this manufactured image manipulation.

This human trait is, of course, evident in our spiritual lives as well. We've substituted other kinds of proof for the proof God is looking for. In John 15:8 Jesus said, "This is to my Father's glory, that you bear much fruit, showing yourselves to be my disciples." We must show ourselves to be what we say we are, by bearing fruit.

For many years a pudding company built their advertising around the phrase, "The proof is in the pudding." Whatever was advertised or promised on the box, the only proof was in actually tasting the pudding.

When it comes to our spiritual lives, the proof is in the fruit. It's required. Fruit is not optional. No matter what we say to others or how many promises we make, the proof is the fruit.

"A tree is recognized by its fruit." Matthew 12:33

The Ultimate Fruit: Love

The word love is perhaps the most used and over-used word in the English language. It is also the most complex and meaningful word we have. Love is what we are to be known for as Christians. But love is so often the last thing we display. We must figure out this ultimate fruit of love. It will take more than rosy poetic descriptions to get there. We may need to get very practical to first see whether we really do love one another, and then get very specific about how we hope to get to the next level in our love.

THE THREE COLORS OF LOVE

The three qualities of God that add up to love are: Truth, Justice and Grace.

In his book, *The 3 Colors of Love*, German church growth researcher Christian Schwarz investigates the quality of love in the church. Love, he tells us, is a matter of reflecting the character of God in our lives. It's part of our connectedness to him. We have already seen that we cannot have growth and fruit without being connected to the "vine." So this makes perfect sense.

Through his research, Schwarz also points out that three qualities frequently used in the Scriptures to describe God overlap one another but each represent a different side of love. In this chapter we will take a look at Schwarz's teaching on love. He gives us a fascinating and practical way of building more love into our lives and the overall life of the church. The three qualities of God that add up to love are: Truth, Justice and Grace.

Going Deeper

If you would like to go further into the subject of love in the church I advise you to read Christian Schwarz's book

The 3 Colors of Love: The Art of Giving and Receiving Justice, Truth and Grace. ChurchSmart Resources © Christian A.Schwarz.

These three words, or rather, their Hebrew counterparts, are found clustered together in several psalms describing God (Psalm 33:4-5; 36:5-6; 40:10; 88:11-12; 98:2-3; 119:75-76). It seems that when the psalmist wants to describe God in a threefold way, these three concepts are the immediate choice. And it makes sense when we remember that God is Trinity. God the Father has always been associated with Justice. God the Son is the Truth, which we proclaim for salvation. And God the Holy Spirit works in and through us to offer Grace to those in and outside of the faith. The Trinity signifies Justice, Truth and Grace much like it signifies Father, Son and Holy Spirit. Each person of the Trinity displays all three qualities because they are one, but it is easy for us to emphasize one aspect of God along with just one of these qualities and not all three and in doing so lose balance.

In order to love more fully, practice the kind of love that doesn't always come naturally.

But there lies our problem. When we determine that we do not love, it is often because we overemphasize one part of love and exclude another. Those of us who are all about truth and justice seek to right wrongs, to do right, and to make things fair. And we point out the absolute truth of Jesus Christ as our Savior. Yet we may still lack the grace portion of love. We may only meet physical needs and not offer the grace to overcome spiritual needs. And we use the truth as a sledgehammer without offering it in grace. You might call that speaking the truth without grace (love). This results in a merciless love.

In the same way those of us who are all about grace and truth communicate the truth of Jesus Christ, and we offer it with grace to all who would accept the open forgiveness of God. Yet we may still lack the justice portion of love. We forget to show genuine compassion and work toward just solutions for those in need. We focus only on communicating the truth. This results in an unjust love.

And those of us who are all about grace and justice offer forgiveness and grace to others for anything and everything, and we have great compassion for the situation of others. Yet we may still lack the truth portion of love. People receive forgiveness and compassion but never hear the truth that saves them. This results in a deceiving love.

Which kind of love do you gravitate toward and which one do you run from? In order to love one another more fully, you must practice the kind of love that doesn't always come naturally. This deep sort of love can only be grown within your connectedness to God. In this way, love can be learned.

Spend some time journaling here about the way you love others. Here are some questions to get you started:

•   Do others in the church know that I love them? How would they be sure?

•   Do others outside of my church know that I love them? How would they be sure?

•   Do I have a sense of justice in the way I love people?

•   Do I have a sense of truth in the way I love people?

•   Do I have a sense of grace in the way I love people?

"Love your neighbor as yourself"— Matthew 22:39

Week One
01.02.03.04.05.06.07.
Group Questions

1) What was one of the best invitations you've ever received?

2) Exercise: Read Psalm 1:1-3 on page 6 of the book out loud together as a group. Go back and circle the words that have to do with growing and plants. Now have every one in the group close their eyes while one member reads the verse out loud. Picture what a healthy plant looks like and compare yourself to it. Where are you healthy? Where do you need help?

3) Where do you think you are in the spiritual formation process described in day two?

4) As a group come up with your own definition of "abiding" (Day three):

    Abide:_____
    _____
    _____

5) In what ways do you act more like rechargeable batteries than extension cords (Day four)?

6) When in your life have you felt like you went through a time of God's spiritual pruning (Day five)?

7) Make a long list of the conditions that your group feels produce fruit (Day six):

8) What do you want to be remembered for?

the fruit of the spirit

The fruit of the Spirit is so frequently cited it could be considered familiar to most Christians. As the list rattles off the tongue we even forget to think about what it really means to live out these qualities.

The qualities that make up the fruit of the Spirit are the first place we should start when we consider what a fruitful life looks like. If we're not showing this kind of fruit first, then we'll never have the kind of lives others will be drawn to.

Week Two Memory Verse:

But the fruit of the Spirit is love, joy, peace, patience,
kindness, goodness, faithfulness, gentleness and self-control.
– Galatians 5:22-23

Love in a World of Hate

In Galatians 5:22 Paul talks about several qualities that we as Christians should have as evidence of the Spirit working in our lives. As we've seen, fruit isn't optional. We cannot say, "Well, I don't have the gift of gentleness." Nope, sorry, gentleness is a fruit of the Spirit, and fruit is not optional.

But the fruit of the Spirit is love, joy, peace, patience, kindness, goodness, faithfulness, gentleness and self-control. Galatians 5:22-23

But the fruit of the Spirit is love, joy, peace, patience, kindness, goodness, faithfulness, gentleness and self-control. Galatians 5:22-23

BACK TO THE BASICS: LOVE

We finished our first week speaking of love, and so it is fitting that we launch into our second week talking about love again. If you're already feeling like you've heard enough about love, then beware—you may need to hear more about it than most people. We need to always return to the basics, and nothing is more basic to the way of Jesus Christ than love.

"Love itself has an inborn need to be recognized by its fruits."
Soren Kierkegaard

Our world is full of hate. Instead of love, our world is filled with war, terror, revenge, infighting, jealousy, rivalry, nasty mobs, violent men, deceitful women, angry children and bitter old people. In this world of hate, we need love, the first fruit of the Spirit, more than ever. We will have this quality showing in our lives if we are truly connected to the vine.

EXERCISES IN GOD'S LOVE

Christian Schwarz suggests twelve simple options or exercises[3] that concentrate on different aspects of love, which help us to practically display this fruit in our lives toward other people:

1)	**Fill up with God's Love**—here is the re-emphasis to stay connected in the vine, where "God has poured out his love into our hearts by the Holy Spirit, whom he has given us" (Romans 5:5). Schwarz notes that "if you are a Christian, you don't have to produce love, you merely have to open yourself up to the love of God so that it can flow through you to other people. God's love is the source and the stream. Your contribution is simply to keep the 'channel' intact."[4]

2)	**Love yourself**—1,700 years ago Augustine said "If you can't love yourself, you can't truly love your neighbor." Those words are even more relevant today than they were then. Loving ourselves means finding our identity in Christ and realizing that we are human—and humans are to be loved. All humans.

3)	**Wear other people's glasses**—this is the process of empathy, seeing the world the way another does. Jesus taught us to not only do this for the needy but even for our enemies (Matthew 5:43-47).

4)	**Put an end to spiritual hypocrisy**—this means speaking the truth in love. It's being honest with who we are and who others are, and finding the tactful way to say things how they are. Too often we fake love

SHOWING THE FRUIT OF LOVE

The great philosopher Soren Kierkegaard once said that love is hidden. "However, this hidden life of love is known by its fruits, and love itself has an inborn need to be recognized by its fruits." As we shared last week, the fruits of love are justice, truth and grace. How do we show these fruits of love? How do we know if we've got them or not?

Three of the greatest early apostles each talked about some aspect of love described in the previous chapter. In fact, each of the three emphasized one portion for us and in so doing wove a beautiful balance.

James emphasized the part of love we see as justice. This is true in two ways. First, the book of James is full of calls to the church to live what we believe: "Do not merely listen to the word, and so deceive yourselves. Do what it says" (James 1:22). And later he went so far as to say, "In the same way, faith by itself, if it is not accompanied by action, is dead" (James 2:17). He made it clear that belief is not enough. In a great play of irony, James said that if you tell him you believe there is one God, he'll point out that even the demons believe that—and they are terrified by it, they "shudder" (James 2:19). This, he infers, is more than we do who believe but don't act on it.

James, we would hope, lived this out in his own life. Early church fathers reported that James spent so much time praying in the temple on his knees that he developed huge calluses on them, and his knees became as hard as a camel's. He was nicknamed "old camel knees." Because of his righteous life and ministry, another nickname stuck with James even more: "James the Just." His life and faith provide a great model for us of the justice emphasis within love.

John emphasized the part of love we see as truth. Often the Apostle John is characterized as a gentle and meek person, even portrayed in some classic paintings as almost feminine in his appearance. But the disciple John was vastly different. He was impulsive and demanding, as his title, "Son of Thunder," implies. His writings include some of the boldest records in Scripture. He proclaimed truth and attacked its enemies.

Perhaps John is known by the softer image because his books contain more talk of love than any others in Scripture. But when writing about love, John often emphasized the truth dimension of it: "I have no greater joy than to hear that my children are walking in the truth" (3 John 4), and "If we claim to have fellowship with [God] yet walk in the darkness, we lie and do not live by the truth" (1 John 1:6), and even "For God so loved the world, that he gave his one and only Son, that whoever believes in him shall not perish but have eternal life" (John 3:16). John was a great model of the truth emphasis within love.

Paul emphasized the part of love we see as grace. It is impossible to read Paul's writings or hear his testimony without being con-

by seeming to accommodate others—when in fact it's just for show. And that's not love.

5) **Learn to trust**—part of love is learning to trust others. This means not suspecting the worst from people, assuming they have ulterior motives. Trust builds the environment needed for love to grow.

6) **Make yourself vulnerable**—many couples falling in love come to that point when one feels the need to verbalize it. That very vulnerable moment arrives when one says, "I love you." The responses could come back in a thousand different ways, but just one, "I love you, too" rewards the vulnerability of the expressed love with returned love. Making ourselves vulnerable is a very difficult thing to do—but the rewards are worth it.

7) **Dare to forgive**—a lack of forgiveness is the opposite of love. Nothing is more loving than forgiving a wrong committed against us. Scripture teaches us that we will be forgiven in the same way we forgive others.

8) **Be transparent**—being authentic is the key to transparency. Who we truly are is exposed. Without transparency our love is just for display. It is manufactured, rather than coming from who we are. Being transparent also opens us to be loved for who we are as well, rather than for who we simply seem to be.

9) **Train to actively listen**—we were given one tongue and two ears, and the logic goes that we should use them in the same percentage: listen twice as much as we speak. However, too often we talk twice as much as we listen. Responding with love is

only possible after we truly listen to where someone else is coming from. Most of us need to train ourselves to listen like this.

10)   **Surprise with gifts**—the essence of the best gifts are that they come as a surprise. Expected gifts are more like exchanges: I give you this because you already gave me that. Practice a life full of gift giving and spread the joy.

11)   **Use your humor**—each of us is funny in our own way. We can use humor to lighten the tensions that don't serve good purposes. And know that the humor level in our churches and the love level are strikingly connected. But above all, we need to learn to laugh at ourselves!

12)   **Have a meal together**—few things show how loving a church is more than how often its people eat together. And few things show how much we love our neighbors than how often we eat with them. Having a meal together is perhaps the oldest and most sacred of the simple acts of love and hospitality. Regardless of how we get it done, let's eat together!

fronted by and comforted by the concept of grace. He thought of himself as the least of the apostles because he persecuted the church before his conversion. But he affirmed that, "By the grace of God I am what I am, and his grace to me was not without effect" (1 Corinthians 15:10). Paul's transformation from a violent persecutor of the church to bold missionary for the kingdom was perhaps the greatest example of grace in history.

GRACE SCRIPTURES

More, even, than talking of God's grace in his own life, Paul's writings to others were loaded with grace. In fact, of the 156 times the word grace is used in the New Testament, 100 of them are in the books of Paul. His letters all begin and end with grace, literally. And in between are the most profound statements of grace ever presented:

•   *My grace is sufficient for you, for my power is made perfect in weakness* (2 Corinthians 12:9).

•   *I have been crucified with Christ and I no longer live, but Christ lives in me. The life I live in the body, I live by faith in the Son of God, who loved me and gave himself for me. I do not set aside the grace of God, for if righteousness could be gained through the law, Christ died for nothing!* (Galatians 2:20-21).

•   *But because of his great love for us, God, who is rich in mercy, made us alive with Christ even when we were dead in transgressions—it is by grace you have been saved. And God raised us up with Christ and seated us with him in the heavenly realms in Christ Jesus, in order that in the coming ages he might show the incomparable riches of his grace, expressed in his kindness to us in Christ Jesus. For it is by grace you have been saved, through faith—and this not from yourselves, it is the gift of God—not by works, so that no one can boast. For we are God's workmanship, created in Christ Jesus to do good works, which God prepared in advance for us to do* (Ephesians 2:4-10).

All three of these apostles reached for the same goal. The Apostle James made clear to us that "faith by itself, if it is not accompanied by action, is dead" (James 2:17). The Apostle John focused on the issue by saying, "Let us not love with words or tongue but with actions and in truth" (1 John 3:18). And Paul reiterated the concept in saying, "The only thing that counts is faith expressing itself through love" (Galatians 5:6). As disciples of Jesus Christ our faith plays out in love for others, in a value for justice, and grace in all we do. All three are essential.

Sow for yourselves righteousness, reap the fruit of unfailing love, and break up your un-plowed ground; for it is time to seek the LORD, until he comes and showers righteousness on you. -Hosea 10:12

Joy in a World Chasing Happiness

You need more joy than happiness in your life.

While your happiness comes from self-pleasure, your joy comes from self-less pleasure. Joy and happiness are nearly opposite in their source of focus. You are happy when things are going good for yourself. It is an entirely circumstantial and emotional state. It can change from one minute to the next.

THE JOY OF CHILDBIRTH

There's no better example of joy over happiness than an expectant mother. I can remember vividly my wife's first pregnancy and childbirth. I remember that people said she had that "pregnant mother's glow." She went through all the typical pains and struggles, being uncomfortable carrying this other human being inside of her. The birth affected her, and me, in tremendous ways. In fact, something happened to me during this time that I still have a hard time believing.

There's no better example of joy over happiness than an expectant mother.

Apparently, some men suffer from a certain condition when their wives are pregnant. It's called "sympathy pain." Some get morning sickness. Others have sore backs. It's a somewhat unexplained phenomenon—since it makes no sense. While Kathy was pregnant, I had extreme pains in my hips at the bottom of my back. I had never had this before, but it was excruciating. Kathy looked it up in her medical dictionary and thought I might have sciatica. She noted that sciatica was very common among pregnant women but very uncommon among other types of people. The pain was so unbearable for me that eventually my many-months pregnant wife had to take me to the emergency room. As I entered with this pregnant woman on my arm, people began to stir to get her a wheelchair and admit her. She said, "Oh, no, it's not me, it's my husband." The orderlies looked at me like I was a creature from

The Fruitful Life

another planet and got me a room. In came the doctor and again she went toward my wife who again had to point out that her husband—the #1 wimp over there—was actually in need of medical help. It was one of the most humiliating nights of my life.

But once the real deal delivery happened (and my sympathy pains had vanished, praise the Lord), the pain Kathy suffered surpassed anything I'd experienced or witnessed in my life. But still, once our son was born, Kathy cried big tears of joy. The whole pregnancy and birth was not a "happy" experience at all. In fact, it was a painful one, in part even for both of us. But was it a joyful experience? Absolutely! You see, even in the middle of pain, joy can be an underlying and overcoming fact of life.

COMPLETE JOY

Did you know that the secret path to joy is found in the vine? John 15:9-11 says, "As the Father has loved me, so have I loved you. Now remain in my love. If you obey my commands, you will remain in my love, just as I have obeyed my Father's commands and remain in his love. I have told you this so that my joy may be in you and that your joy may be complete." The key to joy is remaining in Jesus' love, which he flat out tells us here happens when we obey his commands. It doesn't get much simpler than that. Jesus says that he's laying all this out for us so that his joy will be in us, and even more, so that our joy may be complete. I love that! Complete joy!

"I have told you this so that my joy may be in you and that your joy may be complete." – Jesus

Is anyone ever completely happy? Even if they get everything they've ever wanted and all life's circumstances are peachy, they still want more. I think of the little girl who was asked the familiar question, "If you rubbed a magic lamp and a genie came out and granted you three wishes, what would you wish for?" The girl scratched her head contemplating all her amazing options, her eyes sparkling with possibilities. The girl straightened up and said, "First, I would wish for a million dollars. Second, I would wish for a pony. And third I would wish for more wishes."

THE PURSUIT OF JOY

The pursuit of the American dream is a continual process of wishing for more wishes. Our declaration of independence declares "the pursuit of happiness" as among the three chief "inalienable rights." We do have that right. But even the founders knew that "the pursuit" is all that we could be guaranteed.

Nothing physical can give you joy.

When you possess joy, those around you who do not yet know God desire what you've got. They may experience happiness. In fact, at times they may "feel" even happier than you ever do. All sorts of material things give fleeting happiness. Even some drugs can alter your mood to make you "happier." But nothing physical can give you joy. You can make someone else happy. But you cannot give someone else joy. They must make it themselves by actually caring about you more than themselves. Joy is not store-bought. It's always homemade. When others express joy (more than just happiness) when they hear of good things in your life—that is evidence they possess the fruit of the Spirit we call joy. They are selflessly joyful for you. And their joyful investment in you translates into more joy for them!

So people notice this joy in you. They pause in their pursuit of happiness and recognize that you possess a fruit in life they've never tasted. Your joy draws them to you. Even in hard times you still have it, and they know it, and they want it, too. They begin to stop pursuing happiness and start pursuing joy.

Peace in a World of Conflict

You were meant to be a peacemaker not a troublemaker.

There's an interesting new practice these days in North America. A guy sees someone he hasn't caught up with in a while, and he says, "Hey there, bud. You causing trouble?" As you know, the response is rarely, "No, I'm not causing trouble, I'm a peacemaker." Usually the other guy tries to be as cantankerous as possible, saying "Well, I was never so good at not causing trouble." Or: "Nope—trouble just seems to follow me around." Even: "Nope, I'm just a troublemaker."

This may be a trivial practice among buddies who want to give each other the verbal equivalent of a "punch in the arm." However, the reality is that most of us are better at causing trouble than making peace. Trouble seems to follow us around. We are troublemakers at heart.

But God encourages us to be the opposite. During the Sermon on the Mount Jesus said, "Blessed are the peacemakers, for they will be called [children] of God" (Matthew 5:9). Peacemakers spread peace to others rather than trouble. But notice what happens to peacemakers. They are called "[children] of God." Jesus said that when we do as he does he pulls us up beside him and we somehow gain the same benefits he has in the kingdom.

For sure, being a peacemaker results in great fruit for our lives. When we make peace, we do something that identifies us with God's family and Christ's own role in the kingdom of God. In fact, it gives us Christ's position in relation to God—sons and daughters!

PEACE IS FRUIT AND LEADS TO FRUIT

We were meant to not only have peace but to give peace. For centuries there was a common practice in churches to "pass the peace." Many would think it a strange practice today—but everyone turned to each other (much like our "greet each other" practice today) and said, "Peace unto you." Then the person who just received peace would return it, saying, "And peace also unto you." Its formality likely caused its widespread disuse among evangelicals. If not with a formal greeting, how else could we pass peace to each other? Perhaps we came to church in the first place because we were looking for peace—and got it through the minister. Then when we see others in need of peace, we assume it's the minister's job to spread that peace. But we miss out on the blessed beatitude of God when we delegate up to the professionals the job of passing out peace.

> *Peacemakers who sow in peace raise a harvest of righteousness.*
> James 3:18
> *Let us therefore make every effort to do what leads to peace and to mutual edification.*
> Romans 14:19

OUR MESSAGE IS ONE OF PEACE

When those who do not know Christ see us coming, they often see us as troublemakers not peacemakers. The general view, whether accurate or not, of evangelical Christians today is that we are troublemakers. How do we overcome this image problem? Not through controlling the media or shaping a better message to the world. We overcome it by rediscovering that our message was always about the opposite of trouble in the first place. "How beautiful on the mountains are the feet of those who bring good news, who proclaim peace, who bring good tidings, who proclaim salvation, who say to Zion, 'Your God reigns!'" (Isaiah 52:7). Throughout the Old and New Testaments, we are shown that peace is our goal. Both Psalm 34:14 & 1Peter 3:11 instruct us to "seek peace and pursue it." By doing this, we not only change the way we're seen—but those who don't know Christ will actually find the peace they are seeking.

TRUE PEACE MAKES NO SENSE

But don't fool yourself. The peace of God is not something we can logically explain or intellectually pass out to people. We have more people studying the Bible and preaching the Word than at any other time in history. We have schools full of people who know the original languages of Scripture and (they tell us) know the original meanings better than ever before.

Why then is there still so little peace in the world? Because the peace we think about and articulate is one of our own making. Paul advised us so long ago that when we present our requests to God, "The peace of God, which transcends all understanding, will guard your hearts and your minds in Christ Jesus" (Philippians 4:7). We can't intellectualize the peace God gives. We must experience it—then pass it out from not only a protected mind but a protected heart, just as Paul advised.

A WORLD OF PASSING PEACE

The world can only manufacture a passing and limited peace. Every two years my wife becomes engrossed in the Olympic Games. Since she was a young girl, the calendar seemed to rotate around these worldwide athletic events. Now our children and I are into the games almost as much as she is. Our four-year old son can already hum the theme song to the Olympics.

> *The world can only manufacture a passing and limited peace.*

Did you know that there is an old tradition, dating back to the Greek games thousands of years ago, of a declared peace during the games? Of course, the Greeks often warred during the games. But there was an ideal of peace. When the modern games were initiated, this declared worldwide peace was part of the ideal goal again. But two times in the past 100 years the summer games were cancelled because the entire world was at war. And twice in the 1980s many teams boycotted the summer Olympics as the key cold-war cities of Moscow and Los Angeles hosted the games.

Countries do no better at peace-making than individuals. They in fact do worse. In spite of songs of peace, flags of peace, handshake truces, and summits, our hope for peace never has and never will lie in governments or the leadership of mankind. Jesus said as much to us, but we're still trying to do it on our own. Our Savior lived in an age where "Pax Romana" was the motto of the empire. This "Roman Peace" was achieved through constant Roman conquest, subjugation and violence. Jesus knew that the peace of the world was mostly propaganda.

> *Jesus knew that the peace of men was mostly propaganda.*

But never forget, Jesus came from the beginning to bring peace. The angels told the shepherds, "Glory to God in the highest, and on earth peace to men on whom his favor rests" (Luke 2:14). And when Jesus ascended into heaven, peace was again the gift. "Peace I leave with you; my peace I give you. I do not give to you as the world gives. Do not let your hearts be troubled and do not be afraid" (John 14:27). Jesus gives us peace as the fruit of a life lived in him. Now we should give peace away at every turn: between conflicts, with unspoken struggles, with the past, with less-than-peaceful individuals. Make peace when wronged. Make peace a way of life. Then we will not only live in Christ's peace but be living for his peace.

Patience in a World of Hurry

David was just a young shepherd boy tending sheep in the hills when a messenger approached him. The messenger quickly told David that the prophet Samuel was at David's house, examining all of his brothers. None of them passed muster, so David was being summoned also.

David hadn't even been invited to the party. As the youngest son, he was left to do the dirty work out with the sheep while his brothers had the honor of meeting this amazing guest—the most famous man in all of Israel. David ran quickly to the party, which Samuel was holding up. "We won't sit down until he arrives" Samuel told David's father. Samuel knew he was looking for Israel's next king and that none of David's brothers fit God's criteria. David walked in very unprepared for a prestigious party like this—probably dirty from his days out tending the sheep and sleeping under the stars.

As soon as he entered, God told Samuel, "He's the one." Samuel called him over and poured oil on his head. The oil dripped down David's neck, behind his ears and down the edges of his cheeks, meeting on the few hairs he had managed to sprout on the edge of his chin. From there it poured to the ground. Samuel announced that this boy, the youngest brother not even invited to the party, was God's choice to be the next king of Israel!

SITTING THE BENCH

So what happened next? You would expect a huge processional with the new boy-king entering into his castle and sitting on his throne. Did David become king the next day? No. The next year? Nope. Even in the next decade? Sorry, not even then. David would spend decades on the bench, waiting to get into the game. David went back to tending sheep after being anointed. And even when David came to the brink of fame and kinghood, circumstance,

God's will and David's own patience would sit him right back down on the bench.

When David defeated Goliath…he had patience, and didn't usurp King Saul's throne.

When Saul threatened David…he had patience, and didn't threaten him back, but instead, ran away and lost his place in the king's court.

When David had Saul, unaware, cornered in a cave…he had patience and didn't kill him, only cutting a corner of his robe off to show his mercy.

When David had a sleeping Saul, again unaware, at the tip of his spear…he had patience and didn't kill him, only taking his spear and water jug to mark his passing.

Even when David heard of Saul's death…he had patience, not wanting to assume his place too quickly or without mourning the loss of a valued human being.

David sat on the bench year after year, knowing he was chosen by God to be the king and waiting on the Lord's timing to make it happen. David had the fruit of the Spirit we call patience.

RUTHLESSLY REMOVING HURRY FROM LIFE

Author and speaker John Ortberg writes of a mentor he had talked to on the phone. He was asking for advice about his busy life—and getting done all he needed to get done. The answer he received surprised him. The mentor said, "You must start by ruthlessly removing hurry from your life." John paused, wrote that down, saying, "That's good stuff" to himself. Then he asked the mentor for the next bit of advice. The mentor said, "No, that's it, nothing else. Just ruthlessly remove hurry from your life."

"You must start by ruthlessly removing hurry from your life."

How hurried are you? How hurried did Jesus seem to be? How far apart are those two? If you put your hurry level on a scale of 1-10 how high would it be? Now put Jesus on that same scale.

It's time to ruthlessly remove hurry from our lives and find the time for what counts most: the relationships that reap fruit for the Kingdom of God. It takes the fruit of the Spirit we call patience to order our lives like this.

The Fruitful Life

PATIENT EVANGELISM

It could be said that we do not have evangelistic fruit because we aren't taking enough action. This is true in large part, and we need to do something about it. However, our efforts for evangelism are also hurt by our lack of patience.

When interacting with someone who needs Christ, we are prone to fall to one extreme or another. On the one hand, we say nothing about spiritual things in order to keep the conversations comfortable. On the other hand, once we do say something, we throw patience out the window and call them to a commitment immediately. Both extremes are harmful to producing fruit and are caused by our general dislike of discussing spiritual things with someone who does not yet know Christ personally. We dislike those conversations so much we either avoid them altogether or once we're in them we want to get them over with quickly.

The opposite should be true. A conversation about spiritual things with someone who does not yet know Christ personally should become one of the most enjoyable things we ever do, regardless of our spiritual gifts or wiring. It is of utmost importance—and in reality all we're doing is sharing our story of what Christ has done for us…which should be our favorite thing to share anyway.

A conversation about spiritual things with someone who does not yet know Christ personally should become one of the most enjoyable things we ever do, regardless of our spiritual gifts or wiring.

But if we're honest with each other we'll admit that we don't like these conversations much. Why is that? Why do we avoid them then speed through them when they happen? Perhaps it has to do with an over-emphasis on getting a "notch" in our belt for evangelism. Whether it be a sense that "I did my best and now I don't have to worry about it" or "I got another one in the boat," we often make evangelism into a statistical record-race. We need to move from that philosophy to a style of living where we seek out conversations with those who don't know Christ and hope to carry on those conversations over many months, perhaps years, as we "make disciples" out of them. This takes a style of evangelism we could call "patient evangelism."

It doesn't mean we toss boldness or truth-telling to the wayside. But it does mean that we worry more about starting the conversations than ending them. If anything, ending a spiritual conversation with someone who doesn't know Christ, even if they accepted Christ at the end of the conversation, is a bad thing. That new Christian needs more spiritual conversations with you, perhaps till you or they die, as they are discipled and learn to follow Christ. Evangelism isn't about quickly ending spiritual conversations with non-believers while we try to "close the deal." Evangelism is the process of starting and carrying on the conversation about spiritual things with them. Here again the line between evangelism and discipleship is blurred…and it's a good thing. Jesus didn't say "Go, and make converts" or "Go, and teach the already convinced." He said, "Go, and make disciples."

Be patient in your evangelism. You'll make disciples, and have much more fun doing it.

Jesus had a pretty significant To-Do list. If he ever wrote it down on a scroll, it may have looked something like this:

Jesus of Nazareth
My To-Do List:

❑ Humble myself and take on the form of a man, call this the "Incarnation" and try to explain how I'm 100% fully God and fully man to the uneducated masses in Galilee.
❑ Recruit 12 people who will run things after I'm gone and write down all the important things I did. Start with fishermen.
❑ Tell stories that no one will ever forget.
❑ Heal people as often as possible.
❑ Cast out demons occasionally.
❑ Fulfill each and every prophecy ever made about the Messiah.
❑ Keep the big plan a secret from everyone but my inner circle of 100 or so people.
❑ Go to Jerusalem and tick off all the important people so that they make plans to kill me.
❑ Suffer like no one has in history, and offer my life up as a sacrifice, even though I could stop it at any moment by wishing it to be stopped.
❑ Defeat hell and death.
❑ Rise from the dead.
❑ Give parting instructions to the aforementioned disciples.
❑ Do all the above in just 33 years, most of it in the final three.
❑ Build and prepare individual rooms in my Father's house for every single one of my followers who ever lived in all of history.
❑ Remember to come back in a few years and give a vision of the end times to my buddy John.

The Fruitful Life

❑ Answer every prayer of every righteous person in all of history.

And even with a to-do list like this, Jesus still found the time to play with children, relax in the living room with Mary and Lazarus, sleep in the bottom of the boat and build friendships that changed the world. In fact, Jesus did most of the above list through relationships in the first place.

What does your To-Do list look like?

Kindness & Goodness in a Harsh World

Are you good for nothin'?

YOU'RE GOOD... ADMIT IT... YOU'RE GOOD

My Father loves the classic movie "Analyze This" with Robert DeNiro and Billy Crystal. He particularly loves the way DeNiro's Mafia boss character looks at Crystal's therapist character with his index finger wagging and says, "You're good. No, no, no…you're good. Admit it. You're good." So when my Dad comes over to our house, he does the same thing to my son, Max. Grandpa wags that finger and puts his best Italian DeNiro face on and tells Max, "You're good…yes, you are…you're good." This, of course, makes the kid laugh like crazy.

What if God turned toward you with his finger wagging and did the same thing? "You're good…admit it, you're good." That would feel weird—God calling you good. But the Bible tells us that the fruit of connection to his son is flat out goodness. Ephesians 5:9 says, "For the fruit of the light consists in all goodness." If we have the fruit of Christ we will be good.

If you're wondering what you'll be remembered for, don't look at what you're good at. Look at how good you are. Look at who you are good to. Look at what you are good for.

So be good for goodness sake.

If you're wondering what you'll be remembered for, don't look at what you're good at. Look at how good you are. Look at who you are good to. Look at what you are good for.

HOW GOOD YOU ARE

At its core goodness is a quality. Goodness is about your soul, spirit, and character. It's the essence of you. You can't be good on your own. Many who have no relationship with Jesus Christ will tell you they just "live a good life" and "are basically good." You and they know this isn't the case. We all instinctively know that we don't live good lives. We aren't basically good. We're basically bad. Romans 3:23 confirms our belief and the hunch of non-believers: "All have sinned and fall short of the glory of God." So how good you are comes from how connected you are to Christ.

WHO YOU'RE GOOD TO

Whether you have the fruit of the Spirit called goodness in your life can be determined by who you are good to. Are you only good to those that are good to you? Are you good to those you want something from? Are you only good to those for whom it's easy to be good to? It's being good to those that even harm you that sets you apart as being connected to Christ. True evidence of fruit in your life comes from being good to those you can't get anything from. You are good even when you're treated bad. That may sound impossible for you to do. And you're right. You can't do it on your own. That's why it's a fruit of the Spirit, not a quality you develop. If you have trouble being good to certain types of people, pray that God will give you goodness through His Spirit—which he'll do as you become more connected to Christ. If you're selective in whom you are good to, check the effectiveness of your connection.

WHAT YOU'RE GOOD FOR

Are you good for nothing? Or are you good for God? What you're good for is all about motivation. People can sense motivation. Each and every person has a natural inborn motive radar that is beeping whenever you talk to them. This is why nearly every person in the world dislikes telemarketing. The person getting the call knows that the telemarketer is just trying to get them to stay on the phone longer and buy something they don't need. They know that even if the caller seems nice and asks well-phrased questions, they really just want to sell you something in the end. They know the motivation of the telemarketer.

So don't live your life like you're telemarketing Jesus. Don't be good for the wrong reasons. People will pick that up on their motive radar. And there's nothing worse than feeling like you're being sold something by someone who hasn't even bought it themselves.

WHAT DOES IT MEAN TO BE KIND?

Kindness is the natural outgrowth of a good person's spirit. If you are good then you should be kind. There are three ways to ensure you have the fruit of kindness:

An anxious heart weights a man down, but a kind word cheers him up.
– Proverbs 12:25

1.   A KIND HEART—Ensure that your actual heart is kind. Don't only try to think like Christ, feel like him. The more connected you are to Christ, the more his goodness will become yours, not just in your mind but in your whole being. Only when you begin to naturally feel kindness from within will the fruit of the Spirit of kindness be evident.

2.   A KIND WORD—Proverbs 12:25 reminds us that "An anxious heart weights a man down, but a kind word cheers him up." You can help others to have a kind heart with words of kindness. This is more than just saying nice things. Meaningful conversations, true compliments and words of authentic admiration actually build up the hearts of those who worry too much about life.

3.   A KIND ACT—But you must not only feel and say kind things. You live them out! You must live with kind acts to the needy (Proverbs 14:21,31), to the oppressed (Isaiah 58:10) and even to the ungrateful (Luke 6:35). Such acts of kindness make you a compassionate Christian. If you're having trouble seeing evangelistic fruit in your life, then ask yourself how much compassion you are showing to the needy around you . When Paul spoke of the qualities we should exude so much they are like clothes, the first two he listed were "compassion" and "kindness" (Colossians 3:12). Display this fruit of the Spirit and you'll see evangelistic fruit (results) in your life.

Faithfulness in a World of Broken Promises

Jesus never fails.

My Grandfather on my father's side lived in a mobile home park in the mountains of East Pennsylvania when I was a boy. For as long as I can remember, Grandpa seemed to be in failing health. We visited like all families visit—but with the unspoken specter that each time we visited he seemed to be doing worse.

I remember doing a report for school on kidney dialysis. I chose the subject since I had a real life family example to look to with my grandpa going three times a week to get his "blood cleaned." I remember finding out in my research that many people with kidney failure would eventually have to have some of their limbs amputated. Eventually, with his kidney dialysis only going so far and his circulation not improving, Grandpa's legs began to die. They were both amputated right below the knee. He would never walk again without prosthetic limbs, two canes, and a lot of help. Usually he was in a wheelchair.

But Grandpa never let me know the pain that limitation caused him. More than anything else, I remember him smiling all the time. He had this grin that would come over his face whenever he looked at me. A grinning old man with no legs in a wheelchair—that's how I remember him most.

When we visited Grandma and Grandpa's trailer, mom and dad would sleep in the guest bedroom and my brother and I would sleep in the living room. My sleep would be interrupted frequently by the cuckoo clock they had there. They had all kinds of trinkets, paintings and keepsakes on the walls. Above the hallway leading out of the living room there was a little carved block of wood that had some strange markings on it. I couldn't make out what it said at my age. One early morning I was still sleeping in when the cuckoo clock made its multiple chirps at me. I looked up and saw that Grandpa had already gotten up and was in the kitchen, eating cereal and reading his devotions. When he was done he wheeled back

JESUS NEVER FAILS

past my sleeping bag toward the hallway. As he rolled past me, he noticed I was awake and he grinned his Grandpa grin at me as always. I felt bad for him. Why did he have to suffer when he'd given his whole life to serving God? He was such a nice man. When he entered the hallway I looked above him and saw that block of wood above the doorway. For some reason for the first time I understood what the carved block read. It said, "JESUS NEVER FAILS." For years to come, even after Grandpa finally lost his physical battles, whenever I entered my Grandma's home my eyes would immediately lock on those words, the theme of their home.

THE FRUIT OF FAITHFULNESS

We human beings are not naturally faithful people. We're prone to break more promises than we keep. A person of his or her word is an unusual person for sure. Try as we may we eventually let people down.

But God the Father doesn't. Jesus never fails. The Spirit won't let you down. Scripture is full of promises about the faithfulness of God. Here are a few from just one book:

- For great is your love, reaching to the heavens; your faithfulness reaches to the skies (Psalm 57:10).
- I will praise you with the harp for your faithfulness, O my God (Psalm 71:22).
- For the LORD is good and his love endures forever; his faithfulness continues through all generations (Psalm 100:5).
- For great is his love toward us, and the faithfulness of the LORD endures forever (Psalm 117:2).

> *A faithful person in the world stands out like a sore thumb. Be faithful to those around you and opportunities to reap the fruit of evangelism will abound.*

Faithfulness is one of those qualities that is innately Godly. We can't display it on our own. We must have faith in the Faithful One to give us faithfulness.

A faithful person in the world stands out like a sore thumb. Faithfulness gets noticed. And faithful people make the best friends. Be faithful to those around you and opportunities to reap the fruit of evangelism will abound. People will go to you for help because they know you to care and follow through. People will ask you for advice because they see your faithful character. People will start spiritual conversations with you in order to figure out what makes a faithful person like you tick. "Jesus" is of course your answer.

Gentleness & Self-Control in a World of Rage

The way we carry ourselves shows who carries us.

Two more fruits of the Spirit come next: gentleness and self-control. These effects of the Spirit connection in our lives have everything to do with our demeanor. They relate to the way we come across to others. If at times we come across as out of control, then it's a fruit of the Spirit problem. If we come across as harsh, then it's a fruit of the Spirit problem.

We often think of people who are gentle and kind and meek and humble to be weak and spineless. Sometimes those of us who want to appear strong have trouble with the need to appear gentle to others. And those of us who have used a good temper-tantrum to get our way, whether we are 4 years old in the grocery store or 40 years old in the board room, have trouble with the importance of self-control.

HOW JESUS CARRIED HIMSELF

Jesus' life on earth is the best example of the kind of demeanor we should have and the way we should carry ourselves. Jesus epitomized gentleness and self-control. But Jesus was no spineless wimp. In fact, he was in control of everything at all times. Perhaps our concept of self-control and the way Jesus practiced it is the doorway we should walk through first.

Jesus spent a lot of his time responding to traps and tricks that the Pharisees and the teachers of the law set for him. These were temptations to his gentleness and self-control. Jesus knew what was going on—as Scripture sometimes tells us—but that didn't make it any easier. He knew their conniving ways and still restrained himself. If I were in his situation I would have turned a few Pharisees into mustard seeds every few days just out of poor self-control.

Instead, Jesus walked into each and every situation with complete control of himself. But he wasn't a wimp. Being a wimp means you can be easily pushed around. Nobody pushed Jesus around without his consent. Self-control is the opposite of being weak. Only the truly strong can resist the temptation to react with rage rather than respond with gentleness.

LIKE A LAMB TO THE SLAUGHTER

The Old Testament prophet Jeremiah spoke about those that plotted to harm. He said, "I had been like a gentle lamb led to the slaughter; I did not realize that they had plotted against me, saying, 'Let us destroy the tree and its fruit; let us cut him off from the land of the living, that his name be remembered no more'" (Jeremiah 11:19). For thousands of years we have described Jesus in these terms as well. Like a silent gentle lamb, Jesus not only carried himself with dignity to his death—he allowed it to happen when he could have stopped it.

Only the truly strong can resist the temptation to react with rage rather than respond with gentleness.

The irony is that Jeremiah and Jesus' enemies thought they would destroy their fruit by killing them. In fact, their fruit was all the more effective in their persecution. Their finest hours of fruitfulness came at their deepest points of pain. The fruit of gentleness and self-control prevailed over the world of rage around them.

FRUIT THROUGH GENTLENESS

Those around us who do not know Christ personally are reached through a gentle word. The world is a mean place—they face the opposite of gentleness every day at work, on the way to work, from friends and even from family. People are naturally mean to one another. But when we respond to someone's meanness with gentleness—they notice. They see that we respond in a way that is unnatural. At first—this may make them step back. But over time, they know that there's something different about us. The difference is the fruit of the Spirit in our lives. If our connectedness to Christ produces gentleness in us, we will see evangelistic fruit in even the meanest people around us.

FRUIT THROUGH SELF-CONTROL

Those around us are also reached through our self-control. Sometimes our friends who don't have a personal relationship with Christ will test our "religion" by doing this or that to offend us. It's a common tactic. They want to see if we're a hypocrite or not.

My Great-grandfather was an immigrant coal-miner in Pennsylvania. His wife was out shopping one day when a lady invited her to a small group Bible study. Great-grandma had attended the state church in England but had no real religion or relationship with God. She went and that very first night she "got saved," as she put it. She came home and told my Great-grandfather the news. He didn't say much, but thought, "We'll see how long this lasts." Every day when coming home from the coal mine, he would normally take off the black soot-covered boots and clothes before coming in the house and washing up. But right after she told him the "news," he spent a whole week testing her decision. Each day he trudged upstairs and put all his soot-covered clothes right on the nice bed linens. He figured this would set off his wife—she was known for a bit of a temper—and things would go back to normal. Instead, this changed woman showed self-control beyond her own power and without a word cleaned up the mess and went back to preparing dinner. After a week of this test, my Great-grandfather realized there really was something different. He went to the small group Bible study with his wife and "got saved" himself that night.

His own wife's self-control reached him. She exuded this fruit of the Spirit from the get-go, and only by Christ's power in her life. He became the first and best evangelistic fruit of her life: the patriarch of a Godly family legacy of Christ-followers and even many ministers flowing from his family tree. In some ways I am a part of her fruit as well. And it all started with exhibiting the fruit of the Spirit we call self-control.

Week Two
08.09.10.11.12.13.14.
Group Questions

1)   Exercise: Everyone in the group write their favorite kind of fresh fruit on a card or piece of paper, keeping it hidden from the others. Go around the circle, having each person guess the favorite fruit of the person on their right. If possible, explain why you think a particular fruit is a person's favorite. (For example: Apples, because he's a basic kind of guy. Or, concord grapes, because she's sweet on the outside and sour on the inside. Or, pomegranates, because she's so sophisticated. Or, sliced kiwi, because he's such a cut-up. OK, maybe we're going too far here…)

2)   Share which of the 12 "Love Exercises" on pages 36-38 you are going to focus on doing in the coming week. How can you focus your particular love exercise on the non-Christians you know?

3)   How would you describe the difference between joy and happiness? What gives you the most joy? What gives you the most happiness?

4) In what ways can you ruthlessly remove hurry from your life? Are you ever in too much of a hurry to reach out to non-Christians?

5) Which of the nine fruits of the Spirit are easiest for you to display: love, joy, peace, patience, kindness, goodness, faithfulness, gentleness and self-control? Which are hardest for you to display?

6) Which fruit—those that are hard or those that are easy—demonstrates the work of the Spirit in your life?

7) How has God been faithful to you? How do you need him to be faithful in the coming weeks and months?

The Fruit of the Spirit

the fruit of experience

Experience counts. This isn't just true in the job market—this is true when it comes to spiritual things. And when it comes to fruit. The experiences of your life produce the fruit in your life. At the end of your life, experiences are what you'll remember. And what they produced in you—what fruit they grew—is what others will remember.

You have experienced thousands of events in your life already. Some of those have produced fruit—and will continue to in the future. This week we'll take a journey through the fruit of experience. These are the defining experiences of life that shape your fruitfulness. They add up to The Fruitful Life for you.

Week Three Memory Verse:

My brothers, I want you to know that what has happened
to me has made more people know about the good news.
– Philippians 1:12 (WEV)

Being Developed

Who you are is a result of who developed you.

In many ways you are a product of your creator and your environment:

DEVELOPED BY GOD

God developed you before anyone else. In praising God's amazing all-knowing nature, Jeremiah the prophet said, "Before I formed you in the womb I knew you, before you were born I set you apart" (Jeremiah 1:5). And in Psalm 139:13-14 King David writes, "For You created my inmost being; you knit me together in my mother's womb. I praise you because I am fearfully and wonderfully made." God is not only the Great Physician, but apparently he's an obstetrician. God is intimately involved in our physical development from and even before birth.

But it goes beyond even that. The Apostle Paul says to the believers in Galatia, "My dear children, for whom I am again in the pains of childbirth until Christ is formed in you" (Galatians 4:19). God not only oversees your physical birth but also your spiritual one. And it is a matter of Christ's formation in you. The New Living Translation says, "Until Christ is *fully developed* in your lives." (emphasis mine). That idea of development in Christ is what God wants for and from us.

> *For You created my inmost being; you knit me together in my mother's womb. I praise you because I am fearfully and wonderfully made.*
> *Psalm 139:13-14*

DEVELOPED AS A CHILD

Early in life you were developed in ways that stuck with you. Nearly every study on early childhood development stresses more and more how those years, if not prophetic toward your future, are at least predictive toward it. Your parents or guardians, your siblings (if any), your neighborhood friends, your schoolteachers and classmates—all these people are a part of who you became and are still becoming.

DEVELOPED AS A YOUTH

As a teen you had more control over your development. You were able to make more choices about who your influencers were. For sure, once you had chosen them, much of the end product of your teenage development was already assured. But you still had the choices to make. Coaches, teachers and family all developed you in these years. But your friends likely had more influence in your development as a youth than you expected.

DEVELOPED AS AN ADULT

You may be an adult, but you're not done being developed. The people still investing in you today continue to form who you are becoming. Don't worry if you're concerned that you're only what you were. The past is not the only prediction of the future. But be concerned that you *will become* what you're becoming. By that I mean that your current development is a shadow that shows where you'll end up. Everyone can see it coming. So shape it. Make sure you're being developed and formed by those you want to be like, those you admire.

MILESTONES AND MENTORS

Everyone reaches milestones in their lives. These are points along the way that mark your development: You learn to walk. To talk. To count. To read. To write. To sing. To whistle. To wink. To study. To befriend. To drive. To date. To have your first real job. To live on your own. To marry the love of your life. To have a child of your own. The cycle continues. The mile markers pass.

But these milestones tell far from the whole story. You will pass most of them if you get the chance. What sets you apart from others is who developed you. These people are often called "mentors." Mentors matter as much or more than the other milestones of life. So you should keep track of them just like you would mark your height on a doorframe growing up. Use this worksheet below to write down who developed you up to the present and how they did it. Then look into the future and think of those you would like to mentor you as you continue to develop and grow.

What sets you apart from others is who developed you

The Fruitful Life

EARLY LIFE YEARS: HOW HAVE THEY DEVELOPED YOU?

_____   _____
_____   _____
_____   _____
_____   _____

TEEN YEARS: HOW HAVE THEY DEVELOPED YOU?

_____   _____
_____   _____
_____   _____
_____   _____

ADULT YEARS: HOW HAVE THEY DEVELOPED YOU?

_____   _____
_____   _____
_____   _____
_____   _____
_____   _____

JESUS CHRIST: HOW HAS HE DEVELOPED YOU?

_____
_____
_____
_____
_____

FUTURE MENTORS: HOW WOULD YOU LIKE HIM/HER TO DEVELOP YOU?

_____   _____
_____   _____
_____   _____
_____   _____
_____   _____

Responding to Crisis

Nothing reveals your heart or changes it like a crisis.

Going through an intense crisis forces you to show your true colors. What you truly believe comes out. What you're unsure of comes out, too. And you have to figure these things out in the midst of great loss. Crisis is the crucible Christ uses to shape your future fruitfulness.

A FRIEND'S CRISIS

Few things gnaw at you more than seeing a friend go through a crisis. Whatever crisis they face, you feel like you're going through it with them. You feel their pain. But you aren't, in the end, dealing with the crisis directly. That's some of the pain, in fact. You wish you could do more. You see what's happening and you wish you could do something about it. But you can't. You can only *be there* for your friend.

The way you respond to these crises shapes you deeply. You can become bitter and carry the wounds of another. Sometimes you may not get over the crisis even when the friend who went through it is past the whole thing. Or you can respond to these crises with God's compassion and give peace to your friend. You can respond to that crisis by showing more fruit.

A CIRCUMSTANTIAL CRISIS

Few things are as frustrating as a circumstantial crisis. You lose your job. The house is flooded or burned down. Financial or actual hurricanes hit. The stock market crashes or your boat never comes in. It seems like everything is conspiring against you. These are circumstantial crises.

Going Deeper

If the experience of responding to crisis is an area you would like to go deeper into, I suggest Ken Gire's book

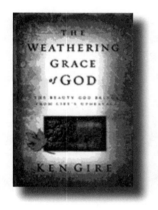

The Weathering Grace of God: The Beauty God Brings from Life's Upheavals. Ann Arbor, MI: Servant Publications © 2001.

How you respond to a crisis of circumstance is important. It shapes your future fruitfulness. For one thing, it shows how much you can handle. Things get tougher as life goes on—if you haven't noticed. And sometimes bad circumstances only become more common the longer you live. Or at least the stakes get higher. Part of overcoming circumstantial crises is the proper perspective. At least circumstances aren't threatening the people you love most. At least you didn't lose a family member.

A FAMILY CRISIS

But sometimes you *do* lose a family member. Few things expose more emotional pain than a family crisis. Unexpected deaths or long torturing sicknesses are often the worst family crises. They can easily embitter you toward others and God. Divorce, infidelity or other marriage problems run a close second to death in the family. These struggles are a crisis that only those connected to Christ can overcome for the better.

A PHYSICAL CRISIS

Few things test your limits like a physical crisis. The whole world may come crashing down around you—but you never know what you can take until your own body is hit. We don't have a real awareness of our body when it's not in pain. You don't think much of your back unless it hurts. In the same way you may take for granted your health and life until some disease or accident threatens both.

A physical crisis that you overcome can drastically shape your fruitfulness. People are amazed to see a man or woman in dire physical straits praise the Lord and remain full of joy (rather than trivial happiness, remember). After you've gone through the valley of death, you can have full confidence that God will use you to bear even more fruit.

A SPIRITUAL CRISIS

Nothing changes your view of the world like a spiritual crisis. Beyond all of these other crises lies this still greater valley. Sometimes a spiritual crisis is caused by one or many of the above crises acting in concert together to push you over the edge. When in a spiritual crisis, you begin to question God. You begin to wonder why he does what he does. You wonder if he's even there. And if he is there, you wonder if he is, in fact, a cruel God. Most people will come to some point in life where they will have a spiritual crisis. This is where the rubber of your faith meets the road. Some don't make it out with any faith at all in the end. But those that do are the most fruitful of all. They not only have confidence in their relationship with God—but they have stared over the cliff of non-faith and seen what the alternative actually looks like.

JOB: A STUDY IN RESPONDING TO CRISIS

Few people experience all the above crises at the same time. But in the Old Testament one man did. His name was Job. When Job lost his friends, his cattle (means of income), his family, his physical health, a spiritual crisis began that made him question God. God spoke to Job in the midst of all his pain, and God blessed him and made him more fruitful than ever, doubling and tripling all he ever had.

One other key person in Scripture went through all the categories of crises above: Jesus. His heart broke over the losses of all those around him. He had nowhere to lay his head and even his clothes were stolen and gambled away. He was bruised, beaten, stabbed, crucified and died. And he lost his family and friends in the process. In the end he had two spiritual crises. He asked that God take the "cup," the suffering, away from him, asking for God to change the plan. And while on the cross he asked, "Why, God, have you forsaken me?" But in the ultimate example of responding to crisis with more fruit than ever—Jesus overcame sin and death and rose from the grave. He paved the path for us to take, and as Paul tells us, we can "rejoice in suffering" because of what it does in us and because it identifies us with Christ.

Getting a "Reality" Experience

Our view of the world could use a reality check.

Reality TV has overtaken television in the United States. Even the Emmy Awards, once the bastion of "serious" television, have awards for reality television and have all but resigned to the fact that many of the "stars" of TV are now regular people chosen from the public and placed in front of the camera in stressful situations.

While many of us bemoan this trend, the ratings don't lie: millions of people tune in every week to see regular people divulge their inner feelings and get themselves into a relational mess with other regular people. They call it "reality," since that's what it's supposed to represent. But we all know it isn't really reality. We know much of it is doctored or staged or misrepresented or blown out of proportion. We also know it isn't *our* reality. Our reality at that point is sitting in climate-controlled environments with chips and a remote control watching staged reality through that little box on the entertainment center.

THE SIMS—SIMULATED REALITY

If that isn't a bad enough representation of "reality," then think about the videogame The Sims. One year for Christmas I bought this videogame for a family member. We were all at a cabin in the woods in the Amish area of Northern Indiana. We plugged in the video game system and took turns playing this game. It was a hilariously ironic first day. Your character (which you can name after yourself or give a fictitious name) starts off living with his mother and sleeping on the couch. You have to become adept at household chores (which your computer-generated mother refuses to do) and eventually get a job and a place of your own. It's all very "realistic." In fact, if you don't pay the bills, you get in hot water. If you don't bathe, your hygiene becomes so unbearable that people won't talk to you. If you don't get enough sleep, you pass out from exhaustion in the yard. And worst of all, if you don't tell your character to go to the bathroom, you wet yourself, even in the middle of a conversation with your imaginary girlfriend.

For a few hours that first day we were laughing hysterically at this "reality" game. We noted how we would tell the character to do the dishes, but none of us had yet done the dishes from lunch in the real world. We would crack jokes about the condition of our real life bladders compared to our character's. One of us suggested that the young men who actually ARE living with their moms and sleeping on the couch are probably better at making their Sims character successful than they are at making their own lives work.

But after a day of this it got old, as we knew it would. Once we immerse ourselves in imitation reality for too long like that—most of us would just rather live our own lives with all our own troubles. With all our own real life reality.

SHORT TERM REALITY WAKE UP

Every once in a while something comes along that shows us the true reality in the world, and it wakes us up for a bit. I don't think I'll ever forget a Frontline special on PBS that showed the genocide in Uganda in the 90s and the failure of the UN and the West to respond to the obvious need. The movie Schindler's List gripped me and altered my outlook on World War II and the Holocaust. And The Passion of the Christ's depiction of the beating Jesus experienced in the final hours of his life was so disturbing and so real that I can't get the images out of my mind—and I think that's probably a good thing.

But while some say that these kinds of films and shows reveal too much reality, they're actually not far removed from the artificial reality of The Sims or today's reality TV. The reason is the experience.

REAL LIFE EXPERIENCE

I can watch The Passion of the Christ on my DVD from the comfort of my living room—just like I can control my Sims character while drinking a Diet Coke.™ Perhaps nothing is inherently wrong with either of these things. However, if I let my life add up to only those climate-controlled experiences, then I really haven't experienced life at all. How much have I done to ensure the things that happened in Uganda don't happen again—even

It's all about getting real life experience.

The Fruitful Life

though I know all about the problems? How much have I done to root out anti-Semitism in myself and others—even though I know all about the Holocaust now? How much am I doing to make sure people know what pain Christ experienced for them—even though I've seen it on the big screen with people munching popcorn around me?

It's all about getting real life experience, and to do that we need to get way out of our comfort zones. And by way out I mean more than just crossing the street to invite a neighbor to our church or small group. It might mean crossing the globe.

GOING TO THE NATIONS

We've talked of two experiences so far that contribute to our fruitfulness: 1) Being developed by another person, and 2) Responding to crisis in your life. The third experience that makes us more fruitful is a risky one. It involves cross-cultural missions. A cross-cultural mission experience happens when we go with a group of people into a culture other than our own for the purpose of advancing the kingdom of God. Everyone that goes on such a mission points to it as a pivotal and shaping experience in their lives. And just like being developed and responding to crisis, it changes us forever and shapes the kind of fruitful lives we live.

Crossing the street to reach your neighbor doesn't seem like that big of a deal in the grand scheme of things.

When I was just 14 years old I went on a mission trip to Lima, Peru. One day we traveled to the shantytown area of that city. We were astonished at the poverty and living conditions. Entire families were living in huts built from scraps of wood, cloth and cardboard. And it wasn't just a few people. As I got out of the car and turned 360° all I could see were these flimsy and filthy cardboard neighborhoods.

We went to a tiny church in this area and after holding a short service one of our team members, Marcie, brought out a bag. Now, since we had arrived there Marcie had ten kids climbing all over her. She had platinum blond hair, which was so rare for them to see, and the kids were pawing at it constantly. But the bag she pulled out was full of candy she had brought from the States. We started to throw it out to all the kids. Within five minutes the crowd had quadrupled as people spilled in from the streets at the news of free food. But though the bag was big, it wasn't big enough. We had to turn people away. Soon, a small riot was starting. As we filed out of that little church, we passed a short woman with an unclothed baby on her hip. She had her hand outstretched, and I could see her frustration when she was told that we were "all out." As I passed she looked me straight in the eyes from 12 inches away. She held out her hand, then looked at her baby. That experience marked me forever. For sure, we didn't do the wisest things that day and maybe we did more to hurt than help. But regardless, that experience changed my view of the world and actually changed the way I live my life. I now know that, yes, I don't have enough for everybody. But God does.

Have you ever had a cross-cultural experience that changed your view of the world and actually changed the way you live your life? What kind of fruit are you seeing in your life since then? Are you in need of this kind of experience? Don't waste any time. Go this year—and see increasing fruitfulness in your life because of it. Once you do, crossing the street to reach your neighbor doesn't seem like that big of a deal in the grand scheme of things.

Developing Brokenness

If you're broken, God can use you.

If you're not, prepare to be broken.

If you've ever wondered if God just seems to be looking for broken people, you might be on to something. Certainly the hall of heroes in the Bible is no list of perfect people. And when you get to know the backgrounds of the Christians you respect the most, you find they don't always have the perfect pedigree either. God uses broken people. He likes to pick up the pieces and assemble his own puzzle picture, rather than buy the finished product.

> *God uses broken people. He likes to pick up the pieces and assemble his own puzzle picture, rather than buy the finished product.*

Which is a good thing for you and me—because we've got issues. But even more than imperfections, God searches for people with brokenness experiences. He's on the hunt for people that have been broken and developed through, in spite of and because of those experiences.

A DREAM TEAM BUILT ON BROKENNESS

We've stumbled on this truth in our staff at Spring Lake Wesleyan Church. Pastor Dennis Jackson, who often calls us his "dream team," has mused that few on our staff were "sure things" when we hired them. Though we often get great encouragement from our people and praise from those outside of our church for the wonderful team we've assembled, we're scratching our heads a bit because we all know we weren't all-stars when we came here.

In fact, not one of the members of our inner core leaders, which we call the "Ministry Program Team," had done the equivalent role we hired them to do before they came here. That's usually the most important thing people look for in hiring—a track record of success in doing what you're hiring them to do. But not here. Some of our MPT members were in an entirely different field before they started a new role here: a nurse who became a children's minister, a young adult minister turned missions pastor, a church planter turned connections pastor, and a social worker turned worship leader turned small groups pastor turned executive pastor. A few were hired right out of college with no full-time experience at all. Others came from a mixed bag of results in other churches. Some of us came directly from flat-out failures.

But one by one each of these team members came here and launched into an extremely productive ministry in a new area of passion. What did we have that Dennis Jackson was looking for—and that enabled us to succeed in uncharted territory? We were broken.

Pastor Dennis has related it to me this way: "We always ask questions about the breaking experiences those interviewing with us have had. We don't want them to hide these things. Their brokenness shows the character God has developed in them. In fact, we so firmly believe that developing brokenness is a journey we all must take that if a candidate hasn't had a breaking experience, we're a bit worried about hiring them. God might then use our church as their breaking experience—and that's a painful process to enter into without a lot of caution." In all honesty, God doesn't seem to care as much about the things we put on our résumés—successful experiences and education—as he does our brokenness.

There are at least three kinds of brokenness:
1.   Self-inflicted. This is brokenness we bring on ourselves. Sin often causes self-inflicted brokenness.
2.   Circumstantial. This is when the stuff of life comes down on us so hard that we have a "breakdown."
3.   God-orchestrated. Sometimes God actually orders events, experiences and emotions that break us so he can use us in the future. This is a tough one—but after their brokenness experiences, many people will confirm that they believe God orchestrated them.

A BROKEN AND CONTRITE SPIRIT

Psalm 51 explores brokenness more than any other part of Scripture. King David wrote this psalm after experiencing self-inflicted brokenness. He had committed the grievous sins of adultery and conspiracy to commit murder. The prophet Nathan called David out regarding his sin, and David immediately repented, writing, "For I acknowledge my transgressions, and my sin is always before me. Against You, You only, have I sinned, and done this evil in Your sight" (Psalm 51:3-4, NKJV). He implores God to "Make me hear joy and gladness, that the bones You have broken may rejoice" (Psalm 51:8, NKJV). David feels this brokenness deeply—even in his bones.

Then there's the familiar part of the psalm, which has been turned into many hymns and songs. David says, "Create in me a clean heart, O God, and renew a steadfast spirit within me. Do not cast me away from Your presence, and do not take Your Holy Spirit from me. Restore to me the joy of Your salvation, and uphold me by Your generous Spirit" (Psalm 51:10-12, NKJV). How beautiful a picture of not only repentance, but of what God can create in us even after our brokenness!

Earlier in the psalm David states: "Behold, You desire truth in the inward parts, and in the hidden part You will make me to know wisdom" (Psalm 51:6, NKJV). Revealing the "hidden part" is the key to the path of brokenness, which creates wisdom in us. That hidden part isn't touched until we're broken. It takes the sharp edges of brokenness to scrape away the many layers covering it.

The psalm draws to a conclusion with a statement about brokenness that ties it all together: "For You do not desire sacrifice, or else I would give it; You do not delight in burnt offering. The sacrifices of God are a broken spirit, a broken and a contrite heart—these, O God, You will not despise" (Psalm 51:16-17, NKJV). Our brokenness is the sacrifice God seeks. You offer him so many other things, your talents, your treasure and your time. But before any of that, he seeks your broken heart.

NEW BIRTH BROKENNESS

Brokenness is rarely a pretty process, but like a birth, it can be the start of something beautiful

The Hebrew word used for "broken spirit" here can also be translated, "the point of birth."[5] In many ways, until we are broken, we are merely incubating until the right timing for a painful but nonetheless essential entry into the real world. Like the birth of a baby, brokenness is rarely a pretty process, but like a birth, it can be the start of something beautiful.

In *Front Porch Tales,* Hoosier author Phillip Gulley tells a fascinating story. When Gulley was a kid, an old man on his street planted several trees in his front yard. Gulley relates how strange it was to see that the old man never watered the trees at all, but would come out with a rolled-up newspaper and beat the tree trunks when they were just saplings. Gulley thought the old man might be a little off his rocker to say the least. One time he asked the old man why he beat the trees. The old man said, "To get the tree's attention." He believed that coddling the trees when they were young gave them shallow roots and no strength for the storms. Gulley speaks of how he still walks by the property of that old man, now long gone. The trees he saw planted, un-watered and beaten with a newspaper are, in Gulley's words, "Granite strong now. Big and robust. Those trees wake up in the morning and beat their chests and drink their coffee black."[6]

Some of us have had times when we've felt like God was senselessly beating us, like an insane old man with a rolled-up newspaper. Some of us feel like that time is right now. Gulley's tale and Psalm 51 tell us that God wants us to grow into strong, fruitful trees. We won't be able to bear the kind of fruit he plans for us until we're fully broken.

Developing Character

Who do people see in you?

It's not just what people see you doing—it's what they see you as. What people see you as is a way of saying, "what defines you." When people define who you are they are making a short description of your character.

In some cases what defines you is what you're good at: your talents. Your school, church, family, business and other social structures encourage you primarily for what you've done well, not for who you are. Professional athletes are often seen as the most disappointing end product of a system that over-emphasizes and rewards talent with no regard for character.

Character never stops being important.

Talents are temporary in importance. But character counts continuously in life. Character never stops being important. The things you're good at now, you probably won't be so good at when you're old and over the hill. And most people won't care. But—no matter how old or how feeble you get—your character will still matter.

THE KIND OF CHARACTER AWARDS ARE NAMED AFTER

Individual awards—the Heisman Trophy, an MVP medal or the Golden Glove awards—are meant to celebrate what one person does in a year of games. My favorite football player is the quarterback of my hometown team, the Indianapolis Colts. Peyton Manning, like many successful quarterbacks, has shelves full of individual awards to go with his team trophies. But in 2004 ESPN magazine, when rating all quarterbacks in the league, said of Manning: "He's the kind of player they name awards after."[7] That statement took me back a bit—even as much of a fan as I am of the player. Why did they say it? It has more to do with who he is than what he's done.

Peyton Manning himself points to one individual award over all others that he is personally proud of, and that's the Sullivan Award. He says that the Sullivan Award is "given to the top amateur athlete not just for what he does in sports but for what he does in school and in the community. Not every Heisman winner has been a model citizen. The Sullivan people honor you for at least trying to be one, as well as for being a good player. They vote on it for reasons I hold dear." Could it be that they name awards after players for different reasons than they give them? And if so, I wonder, do you live your spiritual life in order to "win" awards rather than to have the kind of character that would cause God to name one after you?

HOW TO DEVELOP CHARACTER

The morning paper never had it as good as when Calvin and Hobbes cartoons were in it. In one of my favorite frames, Calvin's parents are hauling him on a canoeing and camping trip. He's being his usually bratty self and complaining that they won't have all the creature comforts they should on a vacation. His eager dad excitedly says that this kind of vacation is what builds character in people. Calvin crosses his arms in the back seat and says, "Why can't I develop character on a beach somewhere?"

You may want to have good character, but you probably shy away from the things that actually develop it in you. What are the things that will develop your character in such a way that you bear more fruit in life?

SEVEN THINGS THAT DEVELOP CHARACTER:

1.   **Time.** It's a tough truth: the older you get in Christ, the more likely you are to develop character in your life. As time passes you either develop character or you develop bitterness and grudges. Your competency may be sky high—but your character needs to be tested with time. You can't do much about this, other than to wait for it to come. Of course, part of the reason time develops character is simply because you've had more chances to experience the rest of this list.

2.   **Failure.** People who have only succeeded in life often lack the character that comes from losing and learning from it. John Maxwell calls this "failing forward" in his book by the same name. Ironically, one of the most successful ways to develop your character is to forge it in a season of failure.

3.   **Scriptures.** An eager heart toward studying the Bible is a sure sign of character, and it builds character in you like little else. That's not my claim; the Bible itself says so as Luke recounts the difference between two groups of Christians in Acts 17:11: "Now the Bereans

were of more noble character than the Thessalonians, for they received the message with great eagerness and examined the Scriptures every day to see if what Paul said was true."

4. **Faithfulness.** Sometimes just sticking with it when others wouldn't builds and shows your character. Sometimes you need to make a decision to stick with something that seems fruitless just because it's the right thing to do. In the end the fruit that comes from it is the change in you. Ruth is credited with character in the Bible for this stick-to-itiveness. When she was courting Boaz he said to her "All my fellow townsmen know that you are a woman of noble character" (Ruth 3:11). Ruth's character got noticed because of the way she faithfully followed her mother-in-law back to Israel even though her sister-in-law did not. And then she took care of this older woman as though she were her own blood. You can't be 100% faithful in everything—and you don't need to stick with everything you start. But when you do—you develop your character in leaps and bounds.

5. **Change.** Change changes our character. You don't grow in your character by staying the same, externally or internally. Your sinful nature likes things the way they are and fights against change. But God upsets your situation and forces change in you to work on the heart issues that hold you back from developing character and producing fruit. God may in fact be in favor of change for change's sake—even when you are not. Change means increased character and fruit in your life.

6. **Accountability.** Having someone who knows what's going on in your head is the greatest way to work on your character in an ongoing way. You can become blind to the sins and character flaws that hold you back from a fruitful life. Accountability partners will confront flaws you're missing and check your blind spots. Their job is to push your character buttons. If they know your weak areas—really know them—then they ensure that you don't take a break from developing character, even when you're not facing some of the other character-producers on this list.

7. **Enemies.** Jesus spoke clearly about how his followers should treat their enemies (Matthew 5:43-44; Luke 6:27,35). How you treat your enemies clearly reveals the depth of your character. You say you don't have any enemies? Think again. Those who oppose you in any way, those you secretly wish would not do well, those who want the Christian cause to fail: they are all functional enemies. Perhaps you hesitate to frame them in those terms because then you would have to love them? Perhaps you think that making their status more "gray" in your mind will allow for your "gray" attitude and behavior toward them. However, you will never get past your character flaws until you confront the issue of your enemies and overcome the barriers to loving them, praying for them, and sharing Christ with them.

Developing Authenticity

You think about what other people think too much.

Be honest. You dwell on this. Before you go into a room, you wonder how people will think you look. When you're done with a conversation, you replay what you said and wonder how it came across. You, like all people, are worried about what people think.

Some people claim this isn't true. They say that "I don't care what people think." But often they're just cultivating an image as someone that "doesn't care." In fact, even this is part of what they want others to think. Others say whatever they like—they are "straight shooters." But often they're also just cultivating an image as being someone that "speaks their mind" and doesn't hold back. Even those who claim not to care really do care what other people think.

IMAGE MANAGEMENT

Projecting a desired image is a huge focus in today's culture. Politicians gather focus groups, take polls and spend millions on commercials to manage their public image. Corporations make precise public moves that have little to do with their goals or production, all in order to create a desired image. Organizations hire agencies to meticulously cultivate this often fake image. Companies allocate funds and create office branches for the sole reason of image management. And image management seems to work.

Even those who claim not to care really do care what other people think

Because of the desire to become more like the business world every day, the Church is fascinated with this phenomenon. Churches and church people are interested in making sure their image remains positive and untainted. Unlike the things churches usually deal in (prayer, salvation, discipleship, teaching, community), image management is totally and excitingly quantifiable. We can measure our image. So we have adopted image management as the latest appendage to church growth and, more importantly, spiritual leadership.

One of my teachers often said to our class, "Say what you want to say but perception is reality." People often come to our churches not because of a delicate investigation of the truth but because of a shallow perception of our image. And that image is one we plan for them to sense. It's a "managed" image.

But often the perception of things is not the ultimate reality. For instance, the professor that told me that perception is reality is the same one that was caught in an affair with his secretary a few years later. In fact, the perception he projected was not reality. In reality the perception we had of him was delicately and intentionally managed. We were manipulated.

What is your image? Do you consciously cultivate it for some purpose of your own? Whether you do or don't, does your image bring people closer to knowing God? Or does it just make them more likely to appreciate you or even follow you? Is your Christianity partially or even mostly based on the image that you have created for yourself? If so, then it's time for an authenticity boost in the way you see yourself and others see you.

Authenticity is all about humility about yourself and appreciation for others. The Bible even points out that trying to manage your image is selfishness. Philippians 2:3 says, "Don't be selfish; don't live to make a good impression on others. Be humble, thinking of others as better than yourself" (NLT). If you appreciate others and trust them, you can reveal who you really are around them.

REAL: THAT MEANS NOT FAKE

Our senior high student ministry at Spring Lake Wesleyan Church has called their ministry "real" for the past several years. Their banner says: "real. that means not fake." I like the simplicity and stark truth the phrase communicates. It's saying: "We're not a fake ministry, we're not about popularity and show, we are who we are—and that's real."

Perhaps a key to the fruitful life is to live the transparent life first. You can't grow to the next level in your fruitfulness if you're not honest about where you are. Christians put on a false front more in the area of evangelism than any other. Whenever the topic comes up, the excuses come out. They'll do anything except admit, "I haven't reached out with the gospel to anyone in months, maybe years."

> *Psalm 69:32 (NLT)*
> *The humble will see their God at work and be glad. Let all who seek God's help live in joy.*

> *Psalm 138:6 (NLT)*
> *Though the LORD is great, he cares for the humble, but he keeps his distance from the proud.*

> *Matthew 18:4 (NLT)*
> *Therefore, anyone who becomes as humble as this little child is the greatest in the Kingdom of Heaven.*

> *Matthew 23:12 (NLT)*
> *But those who exalt themselves will be humbled, and those who humble themselves will be exalted.*

> *1 Peter 5:6 (NLT)*
> *So humble yourselves under the mighty power of God, and in his good time he will honor you.*

Until you develop authenticity in your life—the kind where you can show yourself to be who you truly are, there will always be a roof on your growth and fruitfulness. "God opposes the proud but gives grace to the humble" (James 4:6). Developing authenticity is the simple process of being who you are and not pretending to be someone you're not.

WAYS TO BE WHO YOU ARE

Start with a group of people with whom you can truly be yourself. Your accountability partner, your spouse, your small group, your neighbor, your brother or sister: these can all be that circle in which you're truly yourself 100%. The most authentic people are those who share everything with someone sometime every week.

When you catch yourself saying something to manage your image, add a more humble remark later in the conversation. Sometimes it might even be necessary to say, "I think I overstated something earlier" or "You know…the reality is that I often feel like I'm not doing that very well." This not only helps you stop faking it—it also builds trust in the people in your group. They'll respect you for dialing it down a notch or sharing what you truly feel.

Experienced Investing

Don't spend your life…invest it.

There are a thousand things you could spend your life doing. And I'm not just speaking about your career. In general a lot of things can pass the time. But few things are true investments in the future.

INVESTING IN KINGDOM STOCK

I took a 13-week financial class with my wife a few years back, and it was great information for us to implement in budgeting, spending and saving. Overall, delayed gratification is the key principle to grasp in finances. The idea is to hold off (delay) purchases we desire in the present until they are more affordable and we have the money to spare in the future. Our desires will still be gratified, just later down the road. All the other financial teaching flowed from this simple principle. Of course, this basic principle is the hardest one to live out as a way of life. We see gratification in here-and-now terms. People can get great financial teaching and still mess up their budgets and credit because of short-term pleasure purchases.

Relationships work in a similar way. When interacting with people, we often are more concerned with gratifying our own needs from them in the short run. Relationally, we spend time with friends, but we don't invest in them. We seek to have our own surface needs met—rather than to take the time and have the conversations that pay rich dividends in the long run.

THREE WAYS TO INVEST IN RELATIONSHIPS

First, investing earlier pays off in the long run. When talking with a new friend, it's best to invest in the important conversations early in the relationship. Everyone knows that investing $1,000 now is better than $2,000 in ten years. In relationships it's the same way. The important conversations have to do with spiritual things. Have you ever made a friend who isn't a believer, then got to a point in your relationship when it was awkward to bring up spiritual things? This is often because you didn't divulge that part of yourself early enough. You didn't invest that little bit of spiritual capital early on in the relationship. So then you're stuck dropping "hints" with them about "going to church" and offering "religious asides" that feel far less than authentic. How much easier and more effective it would have been if you had revealed that part of yourself right away.

We spend time with friends, but we don't invest in them.

Second, remember to diversify your evangelistic portfolio. In financial investments having a bunch of different styles and types of stocks over a long period of time not only decreases risk but also increases returns. It's a key economic theory nearly all finance types espouse. But in spiritual things this is true, too. Instead of putting all your "evangelistic eggs" into one basket—hoping to bring just this one person to Christ— spread them out into a number of different investments. This is important for two reasons: 1) you never know if you're going to plant the seed, water it or reap the fruit (in the terms Paul uses; see 1 Corinthians 3:6). So you should go about planting, watering, reaping and contributing to the process in many people's lives. And 2), it's just more authentic. It doesn't make sense for you to turn on the evangelism button when talking to this or that person but not others. You're a follower of Christ no matter where you are or whom you're with. Go on! Diversify your investment into everyone you know, from your neighbor and co-worker, to your family members and the guy at the gas station.

Third, practice consistency in investing rather than waiting for your ship to come in. In finances, you may have learned to put a little away every time you get a paycheck. While it doesn't look like much, over time it does add up. Sharing your faith with those around you operates the same way. Sometimes believers wait forever for their evangelistic "ship" to come in. They hope and pray for that one big conversation with a non-believer where they can share the whole plan of salvation…and then ask the big question. Most people are frustrated with this method, because it happens so rarely and feels so contrived and pressured. A better way is to invest slowly but surely. You don't need to pull the whole "ship" in during one conversation with unbelieving friends. In fact, they may need 50 conversations to get to the point where they "dock" spiritually and commit to Christ. Each conversation with your friends that don't know Christ is like a paycheck—just pull 10% or more of that conversation out and invest it in spiritual things. Like your real bank account, this kind of investment is guaranteed to add up!

HOW TO TALK ABOUT SPIRITUAL THINGS IN CONVERSATIONS

Sometimes you might shy away from these investments because you don't know where to begin or how to follow through in having a spiritual conversation. Sharing our faith can be understood simply by connecting three stories together. You might give it a try. The three stories are: Your Story, Their Story, and God's Story

The three stories are: Your Story, Their Story, and God's Story.

YOUR STORY

It's hard to argue with first-hand testimony. It's why a "witness" in a criminal case is the most powerful defense or offense. In fact, this is why so many years ago people started to use the term "witnessing" for sharing your spiritual story with non-Christians. It may have fallen out of favor as a term today—but it still means the same thing. You're just sharing what has happened to you spiritually. If nothing has ever happened to you spiritually, then other problems exist. But if you're connected to the vine, then your life has been changed. So when asked or given the opportunity, simply share variations of the following (use the space provided to write out yours, if you haven't yet done this:

1.   What were you like before you accepted Christ? (If you came to know Christ very early in life, you can either share about a time of rebellion or what your life "would have been like" without Christ.)

2.   How did God get your attention? (What was it that caused you to wake up to spiritual things and come to know Christ?)

3.   How did you make a commitment to follow Christ? (What process did you actually go through to make it real for you?)

4. What difference has Christ made in your life? (In what ways has God changed you? How does your life make more sense because of Jesus?)

Going Deeper

If you would like to study the ways that Jesus built relationships and lived the most fruitful life of all read Robert Coleman's book

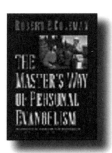

The Master's Way of Personal Evangelism. Wheaton, IL: Good News Publishers © *1997*

THEIR STORY

When it comes to their story you have to listen to where they are coming from. Understand their questions before answering them. If you're worried about becoming an automated "answer man" with your non-Christian friends, then just stop answering questions at all. Say, "I don't know. What do you think?" from time to time. People don't want you to push something on them till they've told their story. A well-placed question from time to time opens this story up to more spiritual things: "So, what's the craziest thing that ever happened to you?" or "What kind of religious upbringing did you have?" or "Do you ever wonder about the purpose of life?" People are spiritual beings by nature—and if you just listen you'll hear their spiritual story over time.

GOD'S STORY

In the end people need to know more than their own story and your story. They need to connect with *the* story: God's story. You might see this as the hardest part of evangelism. In fact, many people don't share their faith because they feel like they don't know enough about the Bible. And the Bible is quite simply "God's story." So this is where things break down. Here's the fix: 1) make every effort to know more about God's story. Don't use a lack of knowledge as an excuse and a de-motivator. Let it charge you up about learning the Word. But also remember 2) that the story is remarkably simple and easy to summarize. Some people have summarized it as simply as: "God loves you and has a wonderful plan for your life." Some have simply quoted Scripture to do it: "God so loved the world that he gave his one and only Son" (John 3:16) or Jesus is "the way and the truth and the life" (John 14:6). The key is to personalize God's story and translate it for people in everyday conversations. What do you think the key to God's story is? Tell people that. And if you don't—you might begin to ask yourself if you really believe the story in the first place.

Week Three
15.16.17.18.19.20.21.
Group Questions

1)   Share around the group some of the names you wrote in the Being Developed Worksheet on page 65.

2)   What are the two or three most significant crisis seasons you've experienced in your life? Are you in one right now? How did you grow in character?

3)   What cross-cultural "reality" experiences have you had? How did you grow in your view of the needs of the world because of these?

4)   What has developed brokenness in you? How do you put up a defense against being broken in your spirit? How do you think brokenness will help you reach out to people?

5)   Which of the seven things that develop character do you need to be more intentional about?

6)   What are the things you like people to think about you that aren't always true? How do you "fake it" in some circles? How real are you with your non-Christian friends? What can you do to be more authentic in all your relationships?

7)   What non-religious friend are you investing in? Who would you like to be investing in? What are you going to do about it?

the fruit of values

Values are about who you are, not just what you do. When it comes to living a fruitful life—it's not just about a list of activities to check off in life regardless of how you feel and think. Actually, it's the opposite. Valuing what is most important in life is key to the fruitful life. Because when these values are really inside of you, then the activities that naturally flow from them will be evident in your life. Your actions follow your attitude. You do what you value.

Week Four Memory Verse:

Then make my joy complete by being like-minded,
having the same love, being one in spirit and purpose.
– Philippians 2:2

What Does It Mean to Be Prayer Immersed?

You are what you value.

Have you ever asked the question, "What will I be remembered for?" There is a fairly simple way to figure out the answer. You will be remembered for the things you valued most. This has a positive angle and a negative one. You could value material things and how much "stuff" you acquire—and when you're gone that's what you'll be remembered for. "Boy, he had a lot of cool stuff." You could value getting things done at work and being successful, and that's what you'll be remembered for. "Man alive, she sure was great at her job."

You will be remembered for the things you value most.

However, these statements point out the dangers of valuing the wrong things in life:

"On their deathbed, no one ever wishes they had spent more time at work and less with their family."

Or, as Billy Graham is credited with saying:

"You never see a U-Haul truck following a hearse."

CHOOSING THE RIGHT VALUES

The first step in being remembered for the right things is to choose the right values. Here's a three-step process to make this happen:

1. Value what Scripture values

It's probably your tendency to start with your own desires and ambitions when it comes to values. But you know that your desires and ambitions can be sinful. So go to the Bible first and discover what it values most. It's hard to miss when you start there.

2. Value what you're passionate about

The Bible is a big book. Can you really "value" every principle in it? You can live by those principles and believe them, but a "value" infers personalization. God allows us great personalization when it comes to living the Christian life. While there are core doctrines we must all believe, God delegates to us the prerogative to develop passion in a personalized area. What floats your boat in the Bible? That's likely what should be your value.

3. Value fruit production

But don't simply value what you're passionate about in the Bible. Value it for the right reasons. Value it for its fruit-producing potential.

In this week's chapters, you'll find seven biblical values that produce fruit. Certainly you can come up with your own values using the above pattern. But these values already pass those three tests, and you can take them and personalize them for yourself.

These statements are not my own. They come out of my community. Spring Lake Wesleyan Church has discussed and debated and determined that these seven statements capture the essence of how God wants us to be remembered. And they produce fruit like little else.

BEING PRAYER IMMERSED

The first fruit-producing value is to be prayer immersed. In chapter 29 we will discuss prayer as a discipline that produces fruit: prayer as an act. But prayer is more than just something we do. And in community it becomes so much more than a program. At our church we've listed five priority programs that are critical to achieving our mission. But prayer is not listed as one of those—because prayer is not a program. It's not a budget item, even if we allocate money toward sparking prayer in the church. Prayer is not a category.

Prayer is a quality. It's a quality in an individual and in a community. We desire to be a community that is immersed in prayer. What does that mean?

PRAYER IMMERSED SCRIPTURES

The Bible is a book of prayer. It relates God's interaction with a people whose only way to communicate with him is prayer. We under-value prayer because we under-value communicating with God. So often we're satisfied to work under our own power and orders. But by valuing prayer we humbly admit our limitations and dependence on God alone.

The following Scriptures speak to prayer in such a way that should compel us to value it:

- ***Ezra 8:23—"So we fasted and petitioned our God about this, and he answered our prayer."*** Prayer is like a "petition," as Ezra relates. This is especially true in community. Like a petition that we pass around and agree to sign, prayer in community is like saying to God, "Lord, we all agree in community that this request aligns with your will, and we pray for an answer."

- ***Matthew 18:19; 21:22—"Again, I tell you that if two of you on earth agree about anything you ask for, it will be done for you by my Father in heaven." "If you be-lieve, you will receive whatever you ask for in prayer."*** These verses explain why many prayer warriors use the phrase "We agree in prayer." Jesus promised us power in agreement. Those who agree can ask for anything. That concept of anything seems unlikely, doesn't it? Hardly anyone fully understands this promise. It seems too good to be true. But that's why we value prayer so much. It has a power we haven't yet fully grasped.

- ***Luke 6:12—"One of those days Jesus went out to a mountainside to pray, and spent the night praying to God."*** If we examine the way Jesus lived his life, we would discover that he valued prayer over anything else. He neglected sleep, preaching, working miracles, the lost and even his disciples to pray. If we truly want to become more like Jesus, we will re-order our world around the value of prayer.

- ***Acts 4:31—"After they prayed, the place where they were meeting was shaken. And they were all filled with the Holy Spirit and spoke the word of God boldly."*** The early believer's prayer caused two effects: 1) they were filled with the Spirit, and 2) they began to speak the word of God in the community with great boldness and fruit! We often value these two results (boldness and fruit) above the over-arching value that caused them in the first place: prayer in community.

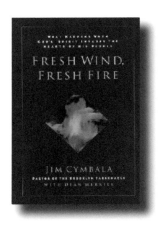
- *Colossians 4:2-5—"Devote yourselves to prayer, being watchful and thankful. And pray for us, too, that God may open a door for our message, so that we may proclaim the mystery of Christ, for which I am in chains. Pray that I may proclaim it clearly, as I should. Be wise in the way you act toward outsiders; make the most of every opportunity."* This is a pillar passage when it comes to bearing fruit in the kingdom through prayer. Paul asks for prayer along three lines: 1) that God would open doors for evangelism, 2) that he would effectively communicate Christ, and 3) that their prayers would make them wise in the way they act toward unbelievers.

- *Hebrews 4:16—"Let us then approach the throne of grace with confidence, so that we may receive mercy and find grace to help us in our time of need."* Many of our prayers can and should involve our own needs. We are instructed to bring them directly to God's throne with confidence…like entering unannounced into the inner courts of a powerful but gracious king —like a prince or princess would! God graciously extends his mercy to us in those situations.

PRAYER IMMERSED QUESTIONS

We can ask ourselves three questions when applying the value of prayer to everyday life. They test whether we are living that value out—or just saying it. People often talk about "unstated" values. These are values a group or individual has but doesn't mention or even admit to. But likewise, many values are stated but unlived. That is the essence of hypocrisy. Asking these questions enables a match between our values and our actual lifestyle:

Have we prayed about this? The question seems so obvious, but it's embarrassing to ask it, because so often we haven't. We move ahead assuming that God would want us to do what we're doing. Or we presume that God has already determined what will happen and our prayers seem trivial. Scripture tells us they are not. Have we prayed about this? If not, it's time to stop, drop and pray.

How have we prayed about this? Specifically? Generally? With passion? Or have we prayed merely in order to check things off a list? A truly prayer-immersed life will involve prayer that is detailed, serious, and full of zeal for God to meet the need.

How long have we prayed? Waiting on God. One of the hardest truths about prayer is that God only answers in his time. Often we forget God's timing. It is a mystery to us. We may grow weary with praying for years—even decades for an answer. But when the answer comes, we are amazed at the timing of God, the Great Timekeeper. And the answer to that prayer is all the more sweet for the many accumulated hours we spent praying for it.

What Does It Mean to Be Biblically Grounded?

Day 23

Without the anchor of Scripture you're drifting.

The current of culture creates a hard pull on you. It causes you to lose sight of the destinations God intends. And our own momentum can sometimes take us beyond where God intended.

My family and I were in Ludington, Michigan, when the grand old "Badger" ferry came in one day. This massive ship, with dozens of cars on it, came into the relatively small harbor and began to turn abruptly to the right. It was barreling toward the dock area, where many people were standing. All of the sudden I heard a great scraping noise. I was beginning to privately worry about the ship being out of control. When a thing that large is moving that fast, not much can stop it.

But then I saw that a massive chain extended from the stern of the ship down into the water. That scraping noise was the sound of the anchor on the bed of the bay, grabbing the ground and helping to stop the boat. And sure enough (they do it multiple times a day, so who am I to worry about them doing it wrong?), the Badger came to a perfect stop right where it needed to.

We need the anchor of Scripture in our lives.

The Bible serves this role in our lives if we value it rightly. It works against the currents of culture that may take us slightly off course. It also slows our momentum toward the excess or even wrong teaching that dev-astates not only our fruit for him, but our own safety.

We need the anchor of Scripture in our lives. We need it like we need the legs we stand on. We call this being biblically grounded. This is the second biblical value that will produce fruit in our lives.

BIBLICALLY GROUNDED SCRIPTURES

The Bible talks about itself often. It is self-referential in the way it values itself. For a revealing exercise, consider what it would be like if the following verses were some bestsell-ing author like Tom Clancy or J. K. Rowling talking about their own book. That would be ridiculous. Only the Bible can talk about itself this way. Because it's the Bible, written by the ultimate Author, the God of all creation.[9]

Those who wonder whether Scripture has authority do more than question this or that pas-sage. They question the Author. The Author of the Bible declares its importance. Few things in life are of ultimate importance. But the Word of God is one of the few. Those who question the Bible's significance are going against the beliefs of thousands of years of God-followers, the Bible's own claims about itself, and what Jesus himself taught.

• *Psalm 119:105—"Your word is a lamp to my feet and a light for my path."* This beauti-fully written psalm points out that the Bible is a source of guidance. When the way seems shrouded in shadow and darkness, the Bible shows the way out.

• *Ezra 7:10—"For Ezra had devoted himself to the study and observance of the Law of the LORD, and to teaching its decrees and laws in Israel."* Ezra was commended for his study and obedience, and for teaching it to others.

• *Isaiah 55:8-11—"'For my thoughts are not your thoughts, neither are your ways my ways,' declares the LORD. 'As the heavens are higher than the earth, so are my ways high-er than your ways and my thoughts than your thoughts. As the rain and the snow come down from heaven, and do not return to it without watering the earth and making it bud and flourish, so that it yields seed for the sower and bread for the eater, so is my word that goes out from my mouth: It will not return to me empty, but will accomplish what I desire and achieve the purpose for which I sent it.'"* God here compares his Word to the process of fruit-bearing. Like rain or snow, the Word falls on us in such a way that it grows us, making us bud and flourish. And we yield fruit—that is, God's Word does not return to him without producing results.

• **2 Timothy 3:16-17**—"All Scripture is God-breathed and is useful for teaching, rebuking, correcting and training in righteousness, so that the [people] of God may be thoroughly equipped for every good work." Paul points out the inspiration and usefulness of the Word of God. It's so inspired, it can be thought as being "breathed out" by God. But it is not some transcendent utterances of our Divinity. It is incredibly useful for all the things that are most important to living a fruitful life. It teaches. It rebukes. It corrects. It trains. It equips us not for some of our good works. It equips us for every single one.

• *Hebrews 4:12*—*"For the word of God is living and active. Sharper than any double-edged sword, it penetrates even to dividing soul and spirit, joints and marrow; it judges the thoughts and attitudes of the heart."* The Bible is not merely a book, nor can we treat it as some general textbook. The Bible is not like some cadaver on the autopsy table of study. In Hebrews, the Bible screams out to us like a living patient about to be cut open by our unkind scalpel, "I'm alive here—treat me like it!" And further, the Bible itself cuts us open, penetrating our soul and spirit and joints and marrow…even to the point of knowing our deepest motivations. We fancy ourselves as trained and reserved surgeons of the Bible—when in fact the Word of God intends to make us the patient. We cut it up brutally, while it repairs us perfectly.

BIBLICALLY GROUNDED QUESTIONS

How much we value the Bible will be put to the test in our everyday lives. When we raise the anchor of Scripture and don't stay biblically grounded, we drift along aimlessly. Even an ordinary, everyday sort of day easily gets out of hand without a bit of time "lowering the anchor." The kind of fruitful life we desire is accomplished through slowing down rather than speeding up. And nothing slows us down like the anchor of Scripture. These questions will help to ensure we're grounded:

Is this consistent with God's Word? We should test our current or planned actions against God's Word. Many times our actions are simply consistent with our own thinking or cultural pressures. The Word of God is far less a philosophical treatise than it is a how-to book. Personally, I'm not much into how-to books. I read the titles and think, "Is that really the only way to do it? Isn't it arrogant of them to tell me how to do everything?" So, I often bristle when the Bible tells me how to live. But we must remember that God is the Author—and his Son walked in our shoes, showing us how to live perfectly. So we should always test our actions against his Word.

Is this truthful? This question gets to the philosophical heart of Scripture. Often when we hear an intriguing teaching or idea, we run with it and apply it to our lives without first testing it against the truth of the Word. I'm especially susceptible to this. Anyone can get a gauge on what I currently believe to be true by just looking at the books and articles I'm currently reading. I'm often embarrassed by what I "used" to think. In the book of Acts, the Berean believers were applauded for testing the truth of Paul's teachings against Scripture (Acts 17:11). Unfortunately, we're often slower to accept the teachings of Scripture than we are of other human beings.

The Bible is the most unexplainable phenomenon of all history.

Will this last? The Bible has often been blithely called "God's Bestseller." Unlike most bestsellers, however, the Bible is the most lasting and true thing on the planet. In the unlikely but humorous prospect of aliens landing on our earth, they would likely be less impressed with our skyscrapers, weapons and transportation than they would with the existence of the Bible, a 4,000-year-old book available in thousands of our languages and being translated into more every day. They would see people of every nation gathering together to hear its words and to learn to live by them. They would wonder where it came from and why it was still around. It is the most unexplainable phenomenon of all history. It is the most lasting thing around—and we should test everything else to see if it's a part of that same lasting legacy or if it will pass away.

THE LARGER THE SHIP THE LARGER THE ANCHOR

A final tip for leaders here: whether you lead a large ministry, a small group, a class of kids or your family's prayers, this applies to you. One thing I've noticed when hanging out at harbors: the larger the ship, the larger its anchor. I've never seen a huge oil tanker with the kind of anchor you would have on a bass fishing boat.

I have, however, seen large ministries and organizations that seem to have a very small scriptural anchor. In fact, I've seen growing ministries exchange a large anchor for a smaller one. As your family, your group, your class or your ministry grows, you need to increase the size of your scriptural anchor. You have much more momentum to take care of now—and your old anchor may no longer be large enough. Practically, this means that the more responsibility you have, the more you should be in God's Word and the more dependent on it you should become.

What Does It Mean to Be God-Led?

Are you going where you're led, or are you just going, and going, and going?

The Energizer™ brand battery has had one of the most enduring commercial images with its "Energizer Bunny™." The sunglass-wearing pink bunny crosses the TV screen with a big battery in its back, mindlessly banging its drum, spinning its wheels and just "keeps going and going and going."

"One way to say yes to the right things is to pre-decide what you're about and live that way." – Dennis Jackson

Do you ever feel a little too much like that bunny? You just keep going and going, and you never quit—or maybe you can't quit? You're a flurry of activity. You run from this meeting to that obligation to that event. You use the restaurant drive-through because you have to. You multi-task. You carry a cell phone so that you can be reached at one obligation by people representing another obligation.

Pastor Dennis Jackson remarked in his Ordinary Day series at our church that "one way to say yes to the right things is to pre-decide what you're about and live that way." What are you about? What do you want to be remembered for? Does it align with what you actually do? Does it align with the obligations you rush to and from?

Or do you feel more like a battery-controlled toy that rolls around on the floor and only changes direction once it hits a wall or some other obstacle. It mindlessly moves about without direction. There's no plan—only action.

BEING GOD-LED

The third biblical value that produces fruit is to be God-led. By seeking God's direction rather than simply moving for motion's sake, we not only keep "going and going and going" but we also keep going in the right direction.

Being God-led is about valuing God's direction over our own opinion. Our opinion about what steps we should take is often based on internal emotions or external pressures. God's clear direction, however, gives us a road map to travel by.

My father used to sign his letters to people with the line, "Keep on keeping on." It was a motivating thought intended to encourage people to "stay the course." Often we need this encouragement because we've either left the course or we never knew the course in the first place. We need to seek God's leading first—then we just have to "keep on keeping on."

GOD-LED SCRIPTURES

We might be able to characterize Scripture as a long record of God's leading. Individuals and communities throughout the Bible experienced God's leading in revelations as stunning as burning bushes (Exodus 3:1-6) and as strange as writing on walls (Daniel 5).[10] But they also experienced God's leading in revelations as subtle as fleeces that were wet in the morning while the ground around them stayed dry (Judges 6:36-40). Or they heard his leading in a quiet whisper, as Elijah did in the cave (1 Kings 19:9-13). Or they heard his leading in his silence, as when Jesus asked that "this cup be taken from me" (Matthew 26:39), and God the Father did not respond. God's leading came in varied ways in the Bible, and still does today:

•   *Proverbs 3:5-6; 16:3—"Trust in the LORD with all your heart and lean not on your own understanding; in all your ways acknowledge him, and he will make your paths straight." "Commit to the LORD whatever you do, and your plans will succeed."* Planning in our own strength makes our paths crooked. It's because we're "leaning" on our own understanding. We need to learn to "lean" on God, which is just another way of saying depend on him.

•   *Isaiah 30:21—"Whether you turn to the right or to the left, your ears will hear a voice behind you, saying 'This is the way; walk in it.'"* Isaiah recorded a marvelous description of what it feels like to receive God's leading. Spiritual maturity includes the process of learning to hear and follow this voice. Some call it conscience—we call it God's grace.

- ***Ephesians 2:10; 5:1***—*"For we are God's workmanship, created in Christ Jesus to do good works, which God prepared in advance for us to do." "Be imitators of God, therefore, as dearly loved children."* God created us to do good works, and he prepared the way for us to do them. We must be "imitators of God" to do these works, of course, because we can't do them in our own power.

- ***Philippians 2:13***—*"For it is God who works in you to will and to act according to his good purpose."* This is an interesting word usage. The word "will" here is as in "willfully." We not only act according to God's will, we choose to do it. Our will is involved. We willfully and willingly choose to act according to God's good purposes in our lives.

- ***1 Peter 2:21***—*"To this you were called, because Christ suffered for you, leaving you an example that you should follow in his steps."* What better way to be God-led than to study the life of Christ and live as he lived!

- ***Colossians 3:17,24***—*"And whatever you do, whether in word or deed, do it all in the name of the Lord Jesus, giving thanks to God the Father through him." "Since you know that you will receive an inheritance from the Lord as a reward. It is the Lord Christ you are serving."* Being God-led involves more than our "religious" or "church" life—it involves all of our beings, every aspect of our lives, and every minute of our days.

GOD-LED QUESTIONS

Is God at work in this? When determining whether or not to be involved in something, this is a helpful question. But it's also a good evaluator of something you're already doing. If you've been at some work for some time and God does not appear to be at work in it, then you have a problem. When God isn't at work in your work, do a double-take.

Are we joining God in his work? When it comes to doing God's work, we often think of ourselves as explorers rather than surfers. That's why we need to ask this question. As explorers we forge a new path; we set out in the direction we choose. Others, we hope, will come behind us. We'll make our mark. However, our role is not to explore but to surf. The wave of God is already coming to shore. God is already moving. We just need to catch the wave. In this role we're more dependent and join his work already in progress.

Is God exalted in this? The point of our activity is to worship God. Everything we do can be an act of worship. If we're not exalting God in what we do, then what we do matters little.

Does this honor God and reflect his glory? The actions we take can honor and reflect who God is. Or not. Asking this question helps us determine if what we are doing points people to God, which is honoring to him and gives him glory.

Are we giving God our all? God honors hard work and persistence. Our faithfulness in what we do is often all that's needed. God leads us to do our best. If we're not doing our best, then we're not God-led.

Are we willingly following? Sometimes we can fall into the trap of following for the wrong reasons. Our obedience comes from the wrong motivation. The key to being God-led is a full surrender of our will to him, following with all our heart, mind and strength.

What Does It Mean to Share Life as a Team in Community?

Don't go it alone.

The English poet John Donne said, "No man is an island." Everyone depends on someone else. However, some people try to be nearly islands in relationships. Like a peninsula, they get by on the least amount of attachment possible, and stick out on their own as much as they can.

How much of life do you live in community? Do you feel like you're on a team? Are you living your life alone or sharing it with others? The Bible shows you the way to live—and it never suggests going it alone. The church is meant to function like a team in community. And as a Christian, you are the church.

BEING A TEAM THAT SHARES LIFE IN COMMUNITY

Many times when we think of friends and the issue of community, we blame others. We wonder why other people haven't reached out to us. We talk about the barriers that other people construct, which keep us from being connected. We blame the team, in effect. We rarely blame ourselves.

But, as the fourth biblical value that produces fruit, it is our responsibility to connect. We must go out of our way to share life. It's our responsibility, not someone else's job.

When we do not live out this value, it affects our fruitfulness as believers in two ways:

We also forget to include those without a relationship with Christ in our community.

1)   The unchurched see the way we treat one another, and they do not long to be a part of it. They see the church as a place of argument and tension, closer to a mob than a team. Without sharing life as a team in community, we hurt the unity reputation we should have as the body of Christ.

2)   We also forget to include in our community those without a relationship with Christ. When we do this, we hurt our chances of truly reaching them. Our past evangelistic ideas usually consisted of "converting" a non-believer then, and only then, bringing them into the fellowship of the church. We've got it all wrong. Just as Christ's example showed us—doing life together with the non-believer is the first step to seeing them on the path to eternal life!

SHARED LIFE AS A TEAM IN COMMUNITY SCRIPTURES

The Bible could be seen as a fascinating tale in four parts: first, God works through the families of the patriarchs to create a community that follows him. Second, God frees this large community of slaves and gives them a promised land on which they rule for hundreds of years as "God's people." Third, God sends his Son as the true and permanent salvation for sin, and his son draws a new people to him out of this community, a team of 12 to start with. Fourth, God raises up a new community of Christ-followers, who send teams to reach the known world with the good news of shared life in Christ.

Community is not simply another value of the story of Scripture. Community is the context of all that is good in the life of Christ. It's not optional. It's intentional.

•   *Acts 2:42-47—"They devoted themselves to the apostles' teaching and to the fellowship, to the breaking of bread and to prayer. Everyone was filled with awe, and many wonders and miraculous signs were done by the apostles. All the believers were together and had everything in common. Selling their possessions and goods, they gave to anyone as he had need. Every day they continued to meet together in the temple courts. They broke bread in their homes and ate together with glad and sincere hearts, praising God and enjoying the favor of all the people. And the Lord added to their number daily those who were being saved."* This famous summary of what the early church was like is fascinating in all its descriptive components. It relates the key elements of sharing life in team and community: devotion to teaching and the community, eating together, praying together, seeing God work, sharing material things and meeting needs with them, meeting together, praising God, enjoying a good reputation, and because of all of the above, God adds to their number daily!

• *Romans 12:4-13—"Just as each of us has one body with many members, and these members do not all have the same function, so in Christ we who are many form one body, and each member belongs to all the others. We have different gifts, according to the grace given us. If a man's gift is prophesying, let him use it in proportion to his faith. If it is serving, let him serve; if it is teaching, let him teach; if it is encouraging, let him encourage; if it is contributing to the needs of others, let him give generously; if it is leadership, let him govern diligently; if it is showing mercy, let him do it cheerfully. Love must be sincere. Hate what is evil; cling to what is good. Be devoted to one another in brotherly love. Honor one another above yourselves. Never be lacking in zeal, but keep your spiritual fervor, serving the Lord. Be joyful in hope, patient in affliction, faithful in prayer. Share with God's people who are in need. Practice hospitality."* Paul here writes to the Roman Christians, whom he has never met, and gives them guidelines for unity in the body. He notes how they should treat one another in the community of Christians called the church. He focuses on brotherly love, honoring one another, zeal for serving the Lord, joy, hope, patience, faithfulness, and prayer. He concludes by reminding the Romans that sharing life with the needy and being hospitable are qualities of all Christians, not something they can choose to opt out of. They are commanded to do these things.

• *1 Corinthians 12:12,18,27—"The body is a unit, though it is made up of many parts; and though all its parts are many, they form one body. So it is with Christ…But in fact God has arranged the parts in the body, every one of them, just as he wanted them to be…Now you are the body of Christ, and each one of you is a part of it."* Paul points out that each part of the body has a different function. Likewise in the church we all have different functions, given to each of us by God. Paul continues in 1 Corinthians with wonderful instructions on how we are to view each other in community. We cannot look down on others or expect them to function in our role—because we are all different. With all our differences God brings us together in perfect harmony, just like a body working together with all its parts.

• *Ephesians 4:1-6—"As a prisoner for the Lord, then, I urge you to live a life worthy of the calling you have received. Be completely humble and gentle; be patient, bearing with one another in love. Make every effort to keep the unity of the Spirit through the bond of peace. There is one body and one Spirit—just as you were called to one hope when you were called—one Lord, one faith, one baptism; one God and Father of all, who is over all and through all and in all."* Here Paul reveals many of the qualities it takes to share life in community. How many times have you seen your community with others break down because of a lack of humility, gentleness or patience? And then we're told to simply "bear with each other" because so often we lack the qualities we need. I love that phrase. We need it in the church. It's almost as if we're told, "Cut each other some slack" or "Give each other a break." Bearing with each other helps us gain the unity of the Spirit we long for—it is the one hope we've been called to together. Don't go it alone!

• *Hebrews 10:23-25—"Let us hold unswervingly to the hope we profess, for he who promised is faithful. And let us consider how we may spur one another on toward love and good deeds. Let us not give up meeting together, as some are in the habit of doing, but let us encourage one another—and all the more as you see the Day approaching."* The role of the church is to hold on to hope and think through how we can encourage each other to love and good deeds. How do we do this? We meet! In these busy times, we are all too willing to complain about meetings and obligations. Yes, we're often over-committed to too many things. But I doubt Jesus would consider our commitment to the community of his fellowship to be over-commitment. We can't share life, become a team and be a community unless we spend time together. We should encourage each other toward a higher commitment to the community of Christ—not let each other off the community hook.

SHARED LIFE AS A TEAM IN COMMUNITY QUESTIONS

Are we doing this together? This simple question helps us check whether we're going it alone. When we experience frustration or a time-crunch, we can ask ourselves if we're doing this task "together." If not, and we're doing it by ourselves, then we've got it all wrong. Life was meant to be done together. I often use the catch phrase "doing life together" to describe this intent. Stop and think how we might do nearly anything we do with others rather than alone. When we do, it adds up to a shared life, instead of a lonely one.

"Only community is forever."

Are relationships developing as we serve? I'm a task-oriented person in many ways. Perhaps you are, too. But in living this value we task-people need to check ourselves on what we're leaving out of the equation. Too often we Christians do the work without doing the relationships. Serving in the congregation and community is a great chance to develop relationships as we go. And this is all the more true in evangelism. When we simply serve with those people we're trying to reach, the relationships and credibility are built up to a point where they want what we've got.

Are we deeply sharing life together? Surface relationships help us feel connected but don't help us truly share life. We can feel lost in a crowd without deep sharing. This is why having a smaller group of individuals we really trust is so important. When we share openly about what has happened to us in the past and what is currently happening in our heart, we go to another level in community, one that is so rewarding we wonder why we hesitated to take the risk in the first place.

Are we using our God-given gifts? Our gifts build up the church and its relationships. Not using them harms the church. When my wife and I started our first church plant, we had a visitor early in the process. Her name was Laura. I knew Laura from the university we both attended. She always seemed to be a very critical and harsh person to me. I thought she disliked many people—but especially me. I was very worried about her coming into our church. But she attended a gifts class we called "S.H.A.P.E." where she learned that she had the spiritual gift of discernment. This gift gives a Christian the ability to spot right and wrong, good and bad motives. Believing in gifts as we did, we took a risk and put Laura on our teaching team, evaluating and helping to form our preaching! So I invited this woman, whom I saw as critical and harsh, to tell me what she thought about my messages each week! You wouldn't believe the change. Instead of being critical and harsh, Laura finally had the forum to use her gift, and she was constructive and helpful. In fact, she became one of the most encouraging people in the church to me after that point! That's the beauty of gifts when they are mobilized as a team in community.

What Does It Mean To Be Encouraging and Joy-Filled?

Do people like to be around you?

When it comes down to it—people like to be around encouraging people who have joy in their lives. If you're a discouraging person, then those who don't know Christ won't want to be around you. They aren't encouraged to know Christ by your attitude or words. If you're depressing, then those who don't know Christ won't want to be around you either. They need to see joy filling your life to want whatever it is you've got.

BEING ENCOURAGING AND JOY-FILLED

But don't worry, you can have joy in your life, the fifth biblical value that produces fruit. Chapter 9 went into detail on this fruit of the Spirit. Review that chapter if you're still struggling. Being joy-filled means not just having joy but showing it. Some people have inner joy but don't value displaying it. But the only way joy can produce fruit is if you show it.

Some personalities may seem more prone to show their joy than others. But a new life in Christ means you can start over and rework your temperament. You can begin by willfully changing the things you say. One way I've done it is to rework the chit-chat I have with people. Instead of saying, "How's it going?" I use a whole different set of phrases, like, "How's your life?" This causes people to pause for a second and consider more than just the moment, but their life. They usually realize their life is going better than their day. Often they ask my question back, and I stop and consider it, too. And I almost always say, "I have a really good life, you know? Some things today aren't working out, but overall I have a lot to be thankful for." I don't cry at the movies, and I don't hug strangers—but I hope little things like this help me show my inner joy.

The Fruit of Values   Day 26

109

Everyone needs encouragement. The church should be a place that values encouraging people in this discouraging world. Make encouraging those around you a priority. But when it comes to encouragement, be a coach or teammate, not a cheerleader. When I played basketball as a kid, we had some great cheerleaders. They cheered us on at every turn. They decorated our lockers before games. They cheered for us before the game. They did little cheers for us to "shoot that ball" or to play "D-Fence." It was very cute. As players, however, their cheering was often more distracting than encouraging. Sometimes they wouldn't be paying attention to the game enough to know that one of their encouraging cheers was happening right after the other team had scored. One time when I was a freshman playing on the varsity team (actually, sitting on the bench for the varsity team), I had two of the cheerleaders come up to me after a game we lost and say, "You played great today, don't worry about it." In fact, I never played a second in that game—I just sat on the bench. Their encouragement didn't have much substance—because they didn't know what was really going on. When you offer encouragement to others, be sure it has substance, that, like a coach or teammate, you know the game and know the best encouraging words to offer.

ENCOURAGING AND JOY-FILLED SCRIPTURES

Few things encourage your heart or fill you with more lasting joy than the Scriptures. This value is not only found in Scripture…it is given by Scripture.

- **Proverbs 12:25—"An anxious heart weighs a man down, but a kind word cheers him up."** This simple proverb reveals the true value of a kind word. What kind of words are you saying each day to your family, neighbors, co-workers and friends? How about the people who serve you at restaurants and stores? Do your words encourage and cheer them up, or weigh them down?

- **Philippians 4:4,8—"Rejoice in the Lord always. I will say it again: Rejoice!" "Finally, brothers, whatever is true, whatever is noble, whatever is right, whatever is pure, whatever is lovely, whatever is admirable—if anything is excellent or praiseworthy—think about such things."** Happiness comes from our outer circumstances, but our joy comes from the things we dwell on. By thinking on the true, noble, right, pure, lovely, admirable, excellent and praiseworthy things, we exhibit joy because of what fills us up. It spills out like an overflowing cup of water to those around us.

- **1 Thessalonians 5:16-18—"Be joyful always; pray continually; give thanks in all circumstances, for this is God's will for you in Christ Jesus."** Giving thanks despite your situation shows your inner joy to those who don't know Christ personally. There is no better witness to knowing God than having this joy-filled attitude. And note that it's not an optional attitude. This passage says that it's "God's will for you in Christ Jesus."

• **Hebrews 3:13—"But encourage one another daily, as long as it is called Today, so that none of you may be hardened by sin's deceitfulness."** Many of you have been hardened by life. Hebrews points out that this hardness comes from the deceit of sin. Apparently, simple daily encouragement is what overcomes this hardness. Do you know someone who doesn't know Christ yet but seems hardened to your conversations about God? Forget trying to win him or her for Christ. Instead, try encouraging that person for a few years, and you'll break through.

ENCOURGING AND JOY-FILLED QUESTIONS

Are we building each other up? It's so easy to tear one another down. When I was in the sixth grade, I had a quick wit and a biting tongue. I would "crack" on other kids and hurt them with my words. My teacher that year was a single Christian man in his 20s. Mr. Jensen lived in a trailer in my part of town. He walked over to my house one day and asked to talk with me. We sat out on my lawn, and he told me how much my cutting words were hurting the other kids in class. I couldn't believe how my simple jokes were hurting the other kids so much that my teacher would walk over to my house and call me on it. I talked with my parents about it, and we devised a little sticker that I put on my desk to remind me to say encouraging rather than unkind things. I believe because Mr. Jensen called me out in the sixth grade my life was changed, and I became someone that valued building people up, not just tearing them down. However, the temptation to bring people down to my level is ever-present. And asking this question helps to ensure I'm an encouraging person to be with, instead of a discouraging person to run away from.

Do we have a positive attitude? Some people just have "additude." These people add something to the room when they enter it. They may not say much, but just their tone and smile and demeanor are positive. Just like the sign for positive—"+"—they add something with their additude. Others just have "subtractitude." They subtract something from the room when they enter it. Their negativity, just like the sign for negative—"-"—subtracts something from every conversation. Be someone with "additude."

Is this increasing our joy? Sometimes we just need to stop what we're doing and ponder this question. Families should do this often. Many times we do something just because we've always done it. Some traditions have value, but if they interfere with the value of being joy-filled, then they need to be adjusted or maybe even scrapped. How many of us have yelled

GOING DEEPER

If you're looking for more on living a more encouraging and joy-filled life read Tom Rath and Don Clifton's practical book

How Full is Your Bucket: Positive Strategies for Work and Life. New York: Gallup Press © 2004.

at our kids to sit still for a Christmas morning picture, and the turmoil ruined the joy of opening presents? In that kind of a situation, we might have to ask, "Is this increasing our joy?" Probably not. Perhaps the kids and their presents are more important than the pictures. In general, we need to do those things that increase our joy. What are they for you?

Are we having fun? Seriously, are we having fun? This is such a rudimentary question we often feel too mature to ask it. If we're not having any fun in life then we have a problem. Have a good time! The fruitful life is fun!

What Does It Mean to Have High Belief and Trust?

It's not just what you believe, it's who you believe in.

It's great to be appreciated, admired and acclaimed, but there's nothing quite like being believed in. You are appreciated for what you are—when someone believes in you it's because of what you could become. You are admired for what you've done—when someone believes in you it's because of what you could do in the future. You are acclaimed for doing something popular—when someone believes in you it's because they see something others don't yet know. So when you're believed in, you are in the highest form of relationship: high belief and trust.

> *How much do you believe in Jesus? That may be the limit to your high belief in others.*

You only trust those you believe in—and when you believe in someone, you should trust them. Believing in someone may be a strong feeling, but trusting them is a decision of the will to release control to them because of your belief in them. But only through the decision to trust will your relationship and that person's own potential be released. If you don't trust anyone—you don't get anywhere close to a fruitful life—and you go nowhere alone.

Like all things in the fruitful life, this sixth biblical value that produces fruit derives from your connection to Christ. How much do you believe in Jesus? That may be the limit to your high belief in others. If you're cynical toward the potential of others, then perhaps you are cynical about what Jesus can do for you. If you're a believer in people, then probably you have high hopes for what Jesus can do and has already done in you. Likewise, the way you trust Jesus determines your ability to trust people. If you've not yet trusted Christ with things as major as your sin and as minor as your feelings—then you won't reveal your sins nor express your feelings to others. Believe in him and trust in him fully. It is the gateway to this value.

BELIEVING IN THE LOST AND TRUSTING THEM TO TAKE THE NEXT STEP

When it comes to the lost, we often view them with a condescending eye. We approach them with a superior spirit. But Christ's example shows us the servant's heart toward the lost. The best example outside of Jesus for me is my grandfather, Leonard Drury. At his funeral nearly two decades ago, I was told of how he "did evangelism." He would visit unbelievers and treat them like gold. He would smile at them at some point in the conversation and simply say, "So, how is your relationship with God going?" He would say this to everyone, no matter how obviously rebellious or irreligious they were. He would say it to people that he knew were not Christians at all and had rejected God. But he believed in them. He believed that no matter where they were, they were somewhere—and all he cared about was encouraging them to take the next step. He believed in them and trusted them to take the next step. They would then open up to him about their spiritual lives. And no matter what the excuses or problems, Grandpa would encourage them and let them know he believed in them. And his belief in the lost made them long to believe what he believed. He continued this practice right up until his death—driving around his trailer park in the mountains of Pennsylvania in his scooter...amputated legs and all. Nothing stood in the way of his life's work: believing in people and trusting them to take the next spiritual step.

HIGH BELIEF AND TRUST SCRIPTURES

The Bible is an incredible account of people God believed in and trusted to respond to and obey him. It's also an account of people who believed in him and trusted him for their salvation. If we follow the example of Scripture, we will be a people with high belief and trust in all our relationships with one another.

• ***1 Samuel 23:16—"And Saul's son Jonathan went to David at Horesh and helped him find strength in God."*** Jonathan exhibited the essence of high belief and trust in his relationship with David. Even though he, Jonathan, was the heir to the throne of Israel, Jonathan knew David was God's choice to be the next king. This friendship of trust was so deep, it was stronger even than family ties—as Jonathan trusted his friend David even more than his own father.

• ***Isaiah 12:2—"Surely God is my salvation; I will trust and not be afraid. The LORD, the LORD, is my strength and my song; he has become my salvation."*** Isaiah records a touchstone verse for our trust in God for our salvation. If we have this kind of trust in God, we have the strength to believe in others and trust them, too.

- **Hebrews 11:6; 12:1**—*"And without faith it is impossible to please God, because anyone who comes to him must believe that he exists and that he rewards those who earnestly seek him." "Therefore, since we are surrounded by such a great cloud of witnesses, let us throw off everything that hinders and the sin that so easily entangles."* Hebrews reminds us that God rewards the seeker—the one that believes that he exists and seeks him. Faith is the key to belief. Our works do not help us find God, our belief does. Plus—wonderful news!—we are believed in ourselves. A great cloud of witnesses in heaven is cheering us on. It's great to be believed in!

HIGH BELIEF AND TRUST QUESTIONS

Are we valuing people? Many times we get caught up in valuing things over people. We can value words over people, too. We can even value what people do over who they are. These are traps that hold us back from the most important thing: the people themselves. It's all about people. If we don't value them, we don't value what God values. Jesus told the story of a shepherd who left 99 sheep to go and rescue one lost sheep (Luke 15:3-7). That story shows just how crucial people really are. It shows how lost people matter to God. People are what should count most to us. And lost people are what should consume our efforts day and night. This question is also about the perceptions of people. Do they feel valued? Do our family members, neighbors, co-workers and friends feel valued by us? How about the lost people in those same groups? How do we show that we value them?

Are we empowering people for effective ministry? The church is a sending agency. It should be all about equipping people and trusting them to do what God has set them apart to do. We should value "giving ministry away" over "having a ministry." A ministry is not a success until real people that leaders believe in are trusted to perform the ministry themselves.

Are we real and authentic? It's sometimes too easy to fake believing in people. But the true test comes in trusting them. Trust is the authenticator of authenticity. If we're not being real and authentic with people, we won't trust them. And if we haven't reached a place of trusting anyone then we may need to consider if we're being real with anyone.

What Does It Mean to Be Love Consumed?

We are all consumed by something.

Have you ever heard of the law of entropy? It's the law of science that says all things in the universe have a tendency to wind down. If you spin a top, it will eventually stop spinning. If you throw a baseball, even on the moon, it won't keep moving forever. In fact the universe itself is slowing down.

Unfortunately our bodies are winding down as well. This is a fact of life I'm learning more and more every year I live. I can still play basketball for a few hours in the afternoon. But the next morning, as I try to get out of bed, I am painfully reminded of the law of entropy ruling my joints and muscles. Our bodies are in fact being physically consumed as we age. They're being used up by life. It's the way it works.

As humans we are like gasoline – we have an innate quality that begs to be consumed.

But in a spiritual way we are also consumed by something. We all have something that consumes us. It's that thing we wake up in the morning thinking about. The thing our minds wander to. That unspeakable desire that seems to creep into our motives. The topic that works itself into our conversations. As humans we have an innate quality that begs to be consumed by something—but we are specifically designed to be consumed by devotion to God.

CONSUMED BUT UNHARMED

After running for his life from the land of Egypt, Moses was tending sheep for his father-in-law on the far side of the desert (Exodus 3). As he turned a corner he came upon a bush that

The Fruitful Life

was on fire. Not so strange, really, lightning may have struck and started the fire. But Moses immediately noticed a dramatic difference between this burning bush and any other. This bush was entirely engulfed in flames but remained unharmed. It did not burn up.

Then the bush began to speak to Moses, or rather, God's angel spoke from within the fire. And history began to be rewritten as God chose this outlaw shepherd to lead his people from slavery to the Promised Land.

God's love burns like that fire, a fire that is designed to entirely consume us but not harm us in the process. We can be consumed by his love—losing ourselves completely to it—and not be burned up by it. Something is still left. In fact, more remains. God's all-consuming love is the seventh and final biblical value that produces fruit.

Indeed, Moses himself became much like that fiery bush. From that day on he burned with the love of God for his people. God didn't need the bush to feed the fire. The fire burned by itself. And likewise God didn't need Moses any more than he needs you and me. We are privileged to be on fire for God, just as Moses was.

LIGHT YOURSELF ON FIRE

John Wesley was once asked to describe why his preaching so effectively reached people for Christ. He explained the process by saying, "I just light myself on fire for God and people come to watch me burn." This compelling vision of a man on fire for God inspires people to this day to follow his example. Our church's mission statement speaks of developing people, but describes these people as having a "consuming devotion." That consuming element is what is missing in the casual believer whose lukewarm assent to God's existence does nothing to bear fruit. But if we allow God to light us on fire for him, people will stop just to watch us burn and great will be our fruit.

If you light yourself on fire for God people will come into your life just to watch you burn.

Never forget, however, that the fuel for that loving fire is found in connection to Christ. Only then will we be able to sustain the fire of love. We cannot do it on our own. We will be burned up—or we will be burned out. But if we stay attached to the vine our fire burns endlessly.

LOVE-CONSUMED SCRIPTURES

The most evident theme in Scripture, its most compelling concept, is that of love. The Bible is an account of unfailing love, the story of love beyond human experience, invention or conception. God's unconditional love makes the Bible a love letter to his people. We open it and find a love we're drawn to like moth to the flame. But unlike that unfortunate moth, once in the flame we find ourselves consumed but not harmed. That unexplainable fire-love is the stuff the truly fruitful life is made of.

• *Matthew 22:36-40—"'Teacher, which is the greatest commandment in the Law?' Jesus replied: 'Love the Lord your God with all your heart and with all your soul and with all your mind. This is the first and greatest commandment. And the second is like it: Love your neighbor as yourself. All the Law and the Prophets hang on these two command-ments.'"* While we don't want to oversimplify or trivialize the complexity of the historical account of Scriptures, there are those moments when Jesus simplified things so much that even children could understand the truth. Here is one of those occasions. Asked directly for the greatest directive in all of the Law, Jesus pulled the first century equivalent of a politician looking directly into the camera, and gave the most important and the second most important command. Loving God with all that we are and loving our neighbors are the essence of what we are to do and be.

• *John 13:35—"By this all men will know that you are my disciples, if you love one another."* Not only is love commanded—it is expected. Love identifies us as true disciples. Love is not an optional value for us. Being love-consumed proves our discipleship and provides for our evangelism. When we love our fellow disciples, it proves in fact that we are disciples. And when those not yet following Christ see that love, it is a testimony that is in fact evangelism.

• *1 Corinthians 13:4-8—"Love is patient, love is kind. It does not envy, it does not boast, it is not proud. It is not rude, it is not self-seeking, it is not easily angered, it keeps no record of wrongs. Love does not delight in evil but rejoices with the truth. It always protects, always trusts, always hopes, always perseveres. Love never fails."* Paul's love pas-sage spins the word love around like a prism and God's light shines through it, showing all the separate colors of love that combine to make it the overarching quality (God is love) of our Father in heaven, and the undercurrent of our life as his followers.

• *Ephesians 4:14-16—"Then we will no longer be infants, tossed back and forth by the waves, and blown here and there by every wind of teaching and by the cunning and craftiness of men in their deceitful scheming. Instead, speaking the truth in love, we will in all things grow up into him who is the Head, that is, Christ. From him the whole body, joined and held together by every supporting ligament, grows and builds itself up in love, as each part does its work."* Love not only cares, but it also cares enough not to look the other way. True love goes beyond the glib "tolerance" our world values. True love accepts people into a community that includes accountability. True acceptance involves accountability. And when we speak truth into other people's lives with love, they are built up. Instead of harming them, such love accepts them, perhaps for the first time in their lives, for who they really are. The world of tolerance allows others to be what they appear to be. The love of acceptance lovingly involves itself in others in order to know who they truly are. And then, as this passage notes, we grow up in Christ, becoming more than we appear to be and more than we were. We become what God wants us to be.

• **Philippians 1:9-11—"And this is my prayer: that your love may abound more and more in knowledge and depth of insight, so that you may be able to discern what is best and may be pure and blameless until the day of Christ, filled with the fruit of righteousness that comes through Jesus Christ—to the glory and praise of God."** Paul makes a tremendous progression here from love to fruit. He writes to the church he started in Philippi and reveals what he prays for them. His core prayer is that their love would grow and abound—you might say to the point of consuming them. And that love would involve knowledge and depth—the kind that involves spiritual discernment in making choices. And he prays that this abounding love would ensure that they are "filled with the fruit" that only comes through Jesus Christ. The goal of all this is to bring glory and praise to God. Don't you love it when Paul summarizes such a massive concept in just a few lines? He describes for us quite simply what it means to have a fruitful life.

• **1 John 3:16-18; 4:7-8—"This is how we know what loves is: Jesus Christ laid down his life for us. And we ought to lay down our lives for our brothers. If anyone has material possessions and sees his brother in need but has no pity on him, how can the love of God be in him? Dear children, let us not love with words or tongue but with actions and in truth." "Dear friends, let us love one another, for love comes from God. Everyone who loves has been born of God and knows God. Whoever does not love does not know God, because God is love."** John defines love by pointing to what Christ did. John notes that love is not just defined by who we are—but by what we do. If we have love, we will do what Jesus did and bravely give up our lives for others. We do this simply by having pity on those in need and giving our material possessions away for them. We can't give lip service to love and not walk the talk. By living it out we show we've been born of God. Born again in fact. Because, and it can't be elaborated on: God is love.

LOVE-CONSUMED QUESTIONS

Does this increase our love for God and each other? Our activities themselves should be love-increasers, not love-reducers. Love reducers are those things that, no matter how we do them, decrease love. Are you a cynic or a critic? Root the cynicism and criticism out of your life and do the things and display the attitudes that increase your love for God and other believers. Replace your cynicism and criticism with excitement and encouragement.

Do we have a deep empathy for those in need? Our love is most tested when we uncover a need in another person. Having empathy for others in need is not a spiritual gift you can opt out of. If you are Christ-like, you will care for others.

Are we accepting of each other with personal accountability? This acceptance is the kind that moves beyond simple tolerance to a willingness to submit to and offer accountability to one another. Asking this question helps us go to another level of love and acceptance with a friend or group of believers, so we are love-consumed together.

Are we choosing to speak the truth in love? This personal accountability is built on speaking the truth in love and walking the path together with our friends in Christ. We cannot speak the truth without loving them enough to walk with them in their growth. Speaking the truth without love is just criticism. The love part is what makes it constructive coaching.

Do we resolve conflicts? Few things test our love more than conflict. We may be love-concerned enough to handle everyday life with those around us. But we must be love-consumed in order to handle conflict with each other. Conflict-resolution isn't possible outside of true love. We may come to a point of agreeing to disagree, or we may negotiate a solution where teamwork can happen again. But without truly loving the other person—having his or her best at heart— we will always carry away a small grudge or a lowered respect after conflict. What makes the church a potentially amazing community is its ability to experience conflict and actually become closer because of its authentic love.

Are we free of gossip? It may seem harmless, but nothing shows a lack of love like gossip. When we speak about someone behind his or her back, we show we don't care for them the way Christ does. Love can't exist in the same room as gossip. They are like oil and water. When we are love-consumed we not only gossip less, we don't gossip at all.

The Fruitful Life

Week Four
22.23.24.25.26.27.28.
Group Questions

1)   What are the things your group values most?

2)   As a group, divide up and reread the Scriptures related to being prayer-immersed and biblically grounded in days 22 and 23 of this week. Discuss how important prayer and the Bible are to your spiritual lives and to bearing fruit.

3)   How strong is your "scriptural anchor" (Day 23)?

4)   What does is mean to you personally to be God-led (Day 24)? How does that play out in your everyday life? How does it make your life different from the unbelievers around you? (Try to answer with more than just "I do…" or "I don't do…" responses.)

5)   Discuss this passage from Hebrews 10:25 from the God's Word Translation: "We should not stop gathering together with other believers, as some of you are doing. Instead, we must continue to encourage each other even more as we see the day of the Lord coming." How do you see the church today living out this command from God?

6)   How encouraging are you to one another? How do you bring joy to your fellow believers?

7)   What high-belief dreams do you have for the people you know who are non-Christians?

the fruit of the disciplines

One of Preacher T. D. Jakes' best lines goes like this: "If you always do what you've always done then you'll always be what you've always been." You'll never show more evangelistic fruit in your life if you keep doing the same things you've always done. None of the spiritual disciplines should be done out of legalistic guilt—they should be done in order to experience the excitement and joy that comes from seeing real fruit. Certain conditions create fruit, and we often call those conditions spiritual disciplines. All the spiritual disciplines that have been invented or taught contribute to your connectedness to the vine and your growth and fruitfulness in it. But the following seven disciplines are practices that some of the most fruitful people in history have had overflowing in their lives. These are the Seven Habits of Highly Fruitful People.

Week Five Memory Verse:

**So then, just as you received Christ Jesus as Lord, continue to live in him.
-- Colossians 2:6**

Prayer

Highly fruitful people pray powerful prayers for the lost.

The first spiritual discipline found in highly fruitful people is prayer. In order for you to become a more fruitful person, you will most likely need to pray more powerfully in the future. Jesus told his disciples, "Look, the fields are white unto the harvest. Pray, then, that the Lord of the harvest will raise up laborers" (Matthew 9:38; 10:2). Jesus' famous words may be well known phrases about prayer. But they are even more powerful when you put them in their correct context, and their context has everything to do with fruit. They tell you four things:

1. THE FRUIT AROUND YOU IS RIPE

When a crop is "white" there's no time to waste. Every stalk is ready to produce its fruit. It may seem overwhelming when you, like Jesus, develop "harvest eyes." It may feel like so many are lost that you can't do much about it. That's why he says that…

2. YOUR FIRST REPONSE SHOULD BE TO PRAY

By praying you overcome the feeling that you can do nothing about the harvest. In fact, it is never true that you can do nothing. You can always do something. The something you can do is pray. And that's a whole lot more than nothing. It's everything. In any situation prayer is always an option. In fact, it's the best option.

One great tool for praying for the harvest is the "My Five" list, a list of five people you have contact with that you are reasonably sure do not have a saving relationship with Jesus Christ. You write these five names on a card and keep it in a prominent place so you can pray over them daily. Our church did this several years ago, and the results were fascinating. People found their hearts changing when it came to the lost people on their cards. Many who had never shared their faith began to do so. People took advantage of every opportunity since they had already put so much time into prayer. And people found that some lost individuals were found on multiple people's cards. God was working from multiple angles to bring these people to himself. Do a "My Five" list today to start praying for the ripe harvest around you.

But Jesus also said that you should pray to "the Lord of the harvest." He said this to point out that…

3. THE HARVEST IS NOT ABOUT YOU

As you live the fruitful life and experience increasing fruitfulness, remember: the fruit in the end is not for you. You surrender the results to God. You are a laborer, but God is the Lord. His lordship here is expressed in unusual terms as the Lord of the Harvest. He presides like a king over his ripe crop being brought into the storehouse. You just pick the fruit.

Many believers find an incredible power in opening up their Bibles and praying Scriptures for the lost. By praying these Scriptures you aren't speaking your own words but the words of the Lord of the Harvest. You might get frustrated when you pray for things and they do not come to pass. And you worry that your prayers may be outside of the will of God—so you pray with less confidence. When praying Scripture you can have the utmost confidence that you are in his will with your words because they are his Words. They are his will written down. In John 15:7 Jesus says, "If you abide in me, and my words abide in you, you will ask what you desire, and it shall be done for you" (John 15:7 NKJV). Abide in his words—use his words in your prayers—and you can jumpstart your own prayers and pray the high-voltage prophetic will of God over the harvest.

Go to these Scriptures and pray them for the lost, maybe even your "My Five" list:
- No one can come to me unless the Father who sent me draws him, and I will raise him up at the last day. John 6:44
- But if from there you seek the LORD your God, you will find him if you look for him with all your heart and with all your soul. Deuteronomy 4:29
- How, then, can they call on the one they have not believed in? And how can they believe in the one of whom they have not heard? And how can they hear without someone preaching to them? And how can they preach unless they are sent? As it is written, "How beautiful are the feet of those who bring good news!" Romans 10:14

- Then he said to his disciples, "The harvest is plentiful but the workers are few. Ask the Lord of the harvest, therefore, to send out workers into his harvest field. Matthew 9:37-38
- Yet to all who received him, to those who believed in his name, he gave the right to become children of God. John 1:12
- Repent, then, and turn to God, so that your sins may be wiped out, that times of refreshing may come from the Lord. Acts 3:19
- That if you confess with your mouth, "Jesus is Lord," and believe in your heart that God raised him from the dead, you will be saved. For it is with your heart that you believe and are justified, and it is with your mouth that you confess and are saved. Romans 10:9-10
- And he died for all, that those who live should no longer live for themselves but for him who died for them and was raised again. 2 Corinthians 5:15

But Jesus does not stop there. He tells you what to ask of the Lord of the Harvest. And it shows that…

4. THE KEY TO THE HARVEST IS MORE LABORERS

You are to ask the Lord to raise up more laborers. He knows that praying for the lost will ensure that your heart will be right and you will make the most of your opportunities. Commenting on the John 15:7 "ask what ye will" verse in his *Explanatory Notes* John Wesley says, "Prayers themselves are a fruit of faith, and they produce more fruit." For sure, prayer is a fruit and it also causes fruit. But in telling you to pray for more laborers, Jesus is also acknowledging that the task is too great for only you. He knows that putting too much of the results on your shoulders would overwhelm you. The key is in mobilizing more laborers.

If you light yourself on fire for God people will come into your life just to watch you burn.

DETERMINING THE EFFECTIVENESS AND POWER OF YOUR PRAYERS

Did you know you could do this? Did you know that the power and effect of your prayers has everything to do with you and little to do with anyone or anything else? Effective prayer never depends on chance. Powerful prayers do not depend on circumstances or other people. The Bible tells you their effectiveness and power depends on—are you ready? You!

James 5:16 says, "The prayer of a righteous [person] is powerful and effective." Do you really think this is true? If you don't, then you have other issues to deal with. If you do, then two things will happen:

First, you'll take your own discipleship more seriously knowing that more hinges on it than your own growth. The health and even the salvation of others may depend on it. When you remember that your prayers have their effectiveness and power rooted in your own connection to the vine, you'll take your own connectedness more seriously.

Second, you'll take your own prayers more seriously—knowing that God pays attention to what you're saying. You'll pray his will more often and pray those things you know to be in his will more carefully.

GOING DEEPER

For a practical and convicting look at building your everyday life around prayer read Bill Hybel's book

Too Busy Not To Pray: Slowing Down to be With God. Downers Grove, IL: InterVarsity Press © 1998.

*Traditionally many people have pointed to between 10-14 *standard* spiritual disciplines. The disciplines in this book are related to the idea of evangelistic fruit, are not as comprehensive, and move beyond the standard lists. For more study on the spiritual disciplines I highly recommend all four of these books: *The Spirit of the Disciplines* (1988) by Dallas Willard, *Celebration of Discipline* (1988) by Richard Foster, *The Life You've Always Wanted* (1997) by John Ortberg, and *With Unveiled Faces* (2005) by Keith Drury, my father.

Day 30 Fasting

When is the last time you did something extreme for God?

The second spiritual discipline found in the lives of highly fruitful people is fasting. Fasting is an extreme thing done for God. Simply defined fasting is the act of doing without something in order to put more focus on God. The most common kind of fast is abstaining from food. The term "fasting" is the opposite of "feasting." When you say "breakfast" you are using two terms: "break" and "fast." That bowl of cereal is breaking the fast you had overnight.

There are several great things that happen when you fast:

BY FASTING YOU GIVE SOMETHING UP FOR SOMETHING BETTER

Except for those with a medical condition requiring it, most of you all could do without one meal from time to time. I myself could do with about one less meal a day, in fact. So when you give up a lunch to pray and fast, you're giving up something that you don't actually need that much. But you gain so much more.

BY FASTING YOU FORCE YOUR PHYSICAL BODY INTO SPIRITUAL ACTIVITY

Usually your religious actions have little to do with your body. But when you fast, you are forcing your physical body to worship. Much like raising your hands when singing a worship song or kneeling when you pray, fasting is a way to worship God with more than just your mind. It is so easy for your spiritual life to be

When you fast, you are forcing your physical body to worship.

The Fruitful Life

all about your mind and soul—and never show in your physical self. Fasting brings all those parts of you together in worship and is the most holistic of the spiritual disciplines.

BY FASTING YOU ROOT OUT THE LUKEWARM ATTITUDES IN YOURSELF

It's nearly impossible to depend on yourself during a fast. If you're fasting from food, you struggle against your hunger and must ask for endurance from God. In this way you are forced to pray and depend on God. You must elevate your "soul over matter" (as opposed to simply "mind over matter"). Fasting is actually the process of allowing your soul to control you instead of your mind or matter! Fasting is not a diet. Fasting is a spiritual exercise that ensures you are not lukewarm in your focus on Christ. It's nearly impossible to be a luke-warm Christian if you fast regularly.

BY FASTING YOU CLEAR AWAY DISTRACTIONS TO LISTEN TO GOD

Admit it; you can be easily distracted from God. But by fasting you clear away distractions and truly listen to God. This may seem illogical to you at first. When I fast from food, won't I be distracted by how hungry I am? Or, When I fast from some other thing in life, won't I think about that all the time instead of God? Well, that's the secret to success in fasting. Those are the things you think about at first. But you use them to prompt yourself to think about God. Those urges remind you, Oh, that's right, I'm fasting. God, help me refocus on you right now. What are you trying to tell me? Fasting is like wearing a massive Technicolor bow on your finger that keeps getting your attention.

BY FASTING YOU OPEN YOURSELF UP TO TEMPTATION

This is actually a good thing for you. Being tempted isn't sin. Sin only occurs once you've given in to temptation. Jesus was "tempt-ed in every way" (Hebrews 4:15) as you are. But he did not give in to sin. When fasting, you'll probably be tempted like no other time. And the temptations are not just the drive-thru's at every fast food joint in town. The temptations can come in waves. Almost like an Olympic athlete in intense training—the harder you fast the harder it can hurt. But just like that athlete—you are building up spiritual muscle under the temptation.

Jesus assumes that you will fast—and he gives instructions for how.

Jesus himself fasted for 40 days and nights before he recruited his disciples and began his years of ministry (Matthew 4:1-11; Mark

FASTING FEAR FACTOR

Fasting is the fundamental faith discipline. It's the entryway to a "fear factor" style extreme life for God. People are attracted by anything that goes against the norm. This is true in your neighborhood and workplace as much as on television. When you live a more extreme life for God you attract people to your kind of life. Why would anyone be attracted to your kind of life if it basically looks the same as their own life. Fasting is one great way to just be different!

Think about this: Is being normal natural to you? I joke with my wife about this. No matter the options, she's always picking "medium". If there are three cup sizes for her soft drink, or three degrees of hot salsa, or three speeds on a machine, she'll always pick medium. Being normal is normal for my wife. Maybe you're normally normal too. Maybe you actually like the color mauve. Maybe you have three pairs of khaki pants. Perhaps you think the Japanese proverb, "The tall grass gets mowed" is a great motto for life. If any of these are true for you then it might be time to mix it up a bit. Determine what next level would get you out of your comfort zone. Risk something for Jesus. Consider fasting as an extreme thing you could do for God. Whatever it is, do something more extreme in your spiritual life—and be transparent with the lost around you while doing it. They'll be attracted to it, you, and in the end, Jesus.

1:12-13; Luke 4:1-13). At the end of this extreme fast, Satan came to him and tempted him with bread, then fame, then power. Jesus resisted each of these temptations by quoting Scriptures he had likely been meditating on during his fast. He resisted the actual presence of the Enemy during and because of his fast.

BY FASTING YOU ARE REWARDED FOR YOUR OBEDIENCE

God rewards this exceptional and extreme practice of believers. Jesus was asked why his disciples weren't fasting openly during their ministry (Matthew 9:14-15). Jesus could have argued with the religious leaders, noting that their fasting was more about others noticing their fast than about concentrating on God. Instead he just noted that his disciples would fast once he was gone after his resurrection. Note who Jesus was talking about: You! You are now the disciples who are living after his resurrection—and should be fasting.

In the sermon on the mount, Jesus said, "When you fast, do not look somber as the hypocrites do, for they disfigure their faces to show men they are fasting…they have received their reward in full" (Matthew 5:16). Note that Jesus says, "…when you fast." He assumes that you will do it—and then he gives instructions for how. Sometimes you may privately think that extreme spiritual disciplines like fasting are unhealthy or unnecessary—because of their public nature. Well,

The Fruitful Life

Jesus asks that you do it—and then shows you how to ensure people won't find out. Finally, he tells you that God, "who sees what is done in secret, will reward you" (Matthew 5:18).

THE POWER OF A FASTING CHURCH

In our church we have the practice of calling the whole church to periodic days of prayer and fasting. We'll set aside a particular date for everyone in the church who is able to pray and fast for a specific purpose. We've found that those issues that we designate a specific day for like this are always resolved. When we've had open staff positions and a struggle in finding God's choice to fill it, God has provided soon after a time of fasting and prayer. When we've had financial shortfall and prayed and fasted about it, God has provided soon after.

While entering into our first capital stewardship campaign for a massive relocation effort, we set aside certain days for prayer and fasting related to that issue. Those days would often come and go with many fasting, but also with many forgetting.

One morning, when the new school year was beginning, a family in our church was getting ready. The mother wanted to start things off right that year and was planning to have a nice big breakfast as a family every morning. Her middle-school daughter said she wasn't going to have breakfast that day. The mother went into a long speech about breakfast being the most important meal of the day. You need to eat breakfast, honey. The daughter quietly responded, "Not today, Mom." Then the mother stressed even harder that she was making a nice big breakfast. Only after repeated challenge did the daughter finally say, "Mom, don't you know it's the day of prayer and fasting?"

We're humbled to think of the power of that kind of obedience in a church. When even our middle-school students are living with exemplary faith and with extreme spiritual disciplines, we know our church is on the right track! Think of the power of a fasting church.

Day 31

Confession

If you confess your sins, God forgives them.

It's one of the most beautiful phrases ever written, don't you agree? The apostle John wrote in his first letter to the church the simple line: "If we confess our sins, he is faithful and just and will forgive us our sins and purify us from all unrighteousness" (1 John 1:9). WOW. This is more than knowing that we are sinners. Deep down we all know this. This is also more than thinking about the idea of forgiveness. That concept alone is revolutionizing. But the idea that our sins won't be held against us? Amazing!

One simple spiritual discipline makes this sort of forgiveness available: confession.

CONFESSION DEFINED

What is confession, this third spiritual discipline, all about? If we are forgiven by it, then we better figure it out. We don't have any other way to deal with our sin, so a lot is riding on it. Confession is the act of admitting our sins. In order to see fruit in our lives, we must cultivate this most basic of behaviors. The fruitful life is gained by living a life of confession. But so often we move away from confession. We may confess sins early in our faith journey—but then later on we are too embarrassed to confess. We think that confession is an act of shame. But rather, confession is an act of confidence and salvation. By confessing our sins we take confidence in the salvation of Christ, rather than depending on our own righteousness to save us. In fact, 1 John 1:9 makes it clear that our faithful and just Lord will cleanse us from our unrighteousness when we confess.

By confessing our sins we take confidence in the salvation of Christ, rather than depending on our own righteousness to save us.

The Fruitful Life

The confessional life has many dimensions. Stretch yourself and live a life of admitting sin in these six dimensions. If you cannot admit your sin in any one of these areas—there is work to be done in you and your community life.

THE SIX DIMENSIONS OF THE CONFESSIONAL LIFE:

1.   A SAVIOR TO CONFESS TO

The first person for you to confess to is Jesus Christ. If you haven't said "I'm sorry" to Jesus, then you haven't genuinely confessed. Perhaps you would rather hide your guilt and not admit your sin to him. But admitting sin is the essence of confession— and he already knows your sin anyway. You might wonder why it's important to confess to Christ, when you accept him initially and along the way in your life. If he already knows why tell him? It is a bit ironic. But it's even more ironic than you think. Usually, when you confess a sin to someone, you are telling them something they don't know. You fear that they will remember that act for the rest of your relationship and hold it against you. But with God it is entirely the other way, upside down, turned around, ironic. God knows all about your sin before you confess it. But once you confess your sins to him, Psalm 103:12 says "As far as the east is from the west, so far has he removed our [sins] from us." So after you confess he truly forgets all about it. God has an amazing quality to be all knowing, but once you let him know, he chooses not to know anymore. You become a new creation to him. Isaiah 43:25 says he blots out your sin and remembers it "no more." Beautiful words! "No more."

> *Admitting sin is the essence of confession —and he already knows your sin anyway.*

2.   A FRIEND TO CONFESS TO

It is also crucial to have a friend to confess your sins to. We've spoken several times about accountability—but here it becomes black and white. If you don't have someone to whom you can confess sin, then you can't open the doorway to true community and authenticity with a broader group. Here's a crazy exercise for you if you don't already have an accountability partner. Find someone of the same sex with whom you already have a fairly good relationship and who is your peer. Get together for the first time and talk about how often you're going to meet, what expectations you have, rules for complete confidentiality, and what you'd like to cover each time you meet. So far this is standard operating procedure. Do at least the previous stuff and get the accountability ball rolling. But now take it to another level and say to your partner, "Next time we get together let's both share a significant past sin in our lives." Many accountability partners take years to get to the point where they can share these kinds of things. But you may not have years to work on your worst sins or deal with your harshest temptations. And you may get in a pattern of not telling your accountability partner everything along the way—a pattern that's hard to break. This sounds scary, I know, but believe it or not, it actually works! If you don't believe me ask MY accountability partner. (On the other hand, don't ask. He knows way too much about me!)

3.   A MENTOR TO CONFESS TO

Sometimes you need more than accountability. Sometimes you need wise advice. Who do you go to in life when you need experienced, sound and wise advice? Those people are likely your informal mentors. It makes sense to develop a relationship with at least one of these mentors that is more intentional—meeting regularly to pick his or her brain and learn from that person. Only one thing will take the relationship to a whole new level: confession. Confess to that mentor that you're not as good as everyone thinks. Reveal to them your incompetencies and failures. Two things will happen: first, you'll quickly find out that your mentor isn't perfect either and may even have the same incompetencies and failures; and second, you open yourself up to being developed in your areas of confession. Before this you weren't being real. You gave your mentor the idea that you were starting at M and needed to move to N, when in reality you were at G and needed to move to H.

4.   A FAMILY TO CONFESS TO

It could be that the key to the confessing life starts at home. We often hurt those closest to us the most. And they are also often the hardest people to ask forgiveness from. I suspect that 3 out of 4 pieces of "emotional baggage" that we all carry around come from what happened to us or what we ourselves caused in our families. We all need to own up to the things we've done in our families. By starting early we can start the pattern right, and not try to act like we have it all together all the time. Parents in particular can confess to their kids when they mess up. The simple "I'm sorry" is a confession that's rarely heard from parents. But every family member can take the initiative, even if it feels too late, to just take the time to say, "I was wrong." If you can't do it here—and you may feel you can't for a long time—then you'll still have family confession work to go back and engage in someday. Why not start now?

5.   A GROUP TO CONFESS TO

Things start to get much trickier when you start to confess to more than just one person. One person you can control easier. One person you can trust more completely. But a group of people is hard to control. Hard to trust. You can't predict what will happen. But the benefits of confessing to a group far outweigh these initial fears. Some small groups get to this point

The Fruitful Life

quickly—others take months and even years. Many others never get there at all. That's okay. Small group environments are not always intimate environments. In fact, people can violate a small group environment by sharing too much too early. I don't suggest going around the circle in your Sunday school class or small group and having everyone share the worst thing they've ever done! Bad idea. However, something beautiful happens when you confess just a little of your struggles and hurt and sin to a group of people. Instead of one person supporting you, you have five or eight or fifteen. And what's more, you break the ice of confession in the group. Here confession is not just a negative act of admitting your faults—it becomes more like pioneering the way for the group. You become the first one to break the confession ice. And often, whether it's right away or over the next few weeks, several people will follow your lead. This all depends on people responding with grace and love to your confession, as Christ would, and being willing to go where no one has gone before.

6.   A CHURCH TO CONFESS TO

When your sin affects more than just yourself and your immediate circle, you might need to confess to your entire church. Few things are harder. But few things can better heal and minister in a broken situation. The principle is that you should confess your sin to those your sin has hurt. If you are a well known member of the church, then you may need to confess to some 100 people. If you are a leader in a ministry area over others, you may need to confess to the whole ministry team. And if you're a leader of a church-wide ministry (or a minister yourself), then the confession should reach the ears of the whole church. Now, there are gentle and responsible ways to do this, and violating and needless ways to do it. The leaders of the church make that call. But offering yourself up to these kinds of confessions is the ultimate act of humility before the church. A friend of mine sent me his restoration testimony recently. He was a youth worker who became involved in an improper and sinful relationship with a girl in his church. Even after they had confessed to Christ and a few others and re-established purity—they found out she was pregnant. You see the sin in fact affected a much larger circle than they had wished, which is so often the case. Sin costs you, but it also costs others—some you may not even think of. So this young man took his brokenness in hand, resigned, and confessed to his entire church. Then he submitted to a multiple-year process of restitution and restoration, and married the young woman who was carrying his child. A broken, sinful and even shameful situation became a restored, pure and even joyful situation. All because confessing our sins to God and his church shows him to be faithful and just, and forgiving of all our sins. He cleanses us!

7.   A COMMUNITY TO CONFESS TO

Donald Miller, author of the book Blue Like Jazz, relates a story from a different perspective when it comes to confession. He and a very small group of Christian friends went to a permissive school in the Pacific Northwest that encouraged extreme lifestyles. The school would have a huge and bizarre party each year where every kind of excess was permitted and celebrated. Students even walked naked around the campus for days. Obviously this was a difficult environment to know how to do evangelism. The fellow students they talked to about their faith would respond with outbursts and hang-ups about the flaws of evangelicals and the sins of the Christian church in history or even in the present. They were getting nowhere and had nearly given up. Then the group decided to put up a "confession booth" in the middle of the common area of campus. They constructed this booth, put up a big sign saying "confession booth" and then took turns waiting for people to come in and talk with them. After a while one brave soul finally went in, wondering what was going on. The Christian on duty proceeded to tell the man that entered that they were going to confess, and he didn't have to participate if he didn't want to. So the Christian began to tell the man that he was sorry for the sins that have been committed in the name of the church throughout the years. He was sorry for the way some Christians had offended people. He was sorry for this and for that. He made a "reverse confession." This wasn't what the unbelieving man had expected— but it had a profound effect. Walls began to come down. Word spread and before long there was a line on that campus to not only hear the confessions of these Christians, but to hear the Gospel with new ears. Ears that were ready to hear because of the authenticity and humility of the Christians in that community.

If you practice these ways to confess your sins, you will see fruit like never before in your life. Live a confessional life—and you will have a fruitful one.

> *Through Jesus, therefore, let us continually offer to God a sacrifice of praise—the fruit of lips that confess his name.* Hebrews 13:15

Day 32

Meditation

What goes in must come out.

Mothers used to be famous for that phrase. "What goes in must come out." Or, "Garbage in, garbage out." They say it to kids watching TV shows they shouldn't or listening to inappropriate lyrics in music. They're saying, be careful little eyes what you see. Be careful little ears what you hear.

In an age where censorship is seen as a cardinal sin, mothers are far less likely to use that phrase. Children of young ages experience filth that is readily accessible and apparently unavoidable. Perhaps we forgot how much that mother's wisdom is true. For sure, the things that enter our eyes and ears must eventually enter our minds and come out of our mouths and our lives. But we so often cry foul to this. "Not necessarily, we say. It's not always the case. We can't blame one behavior on one pattern of input." Well, common sense tells us differently. We know that what we see and hear affects us.

That's the negative side of that truth. But there's a positive side. The positive things we see and hear also affect us. And when it comes to the Bible, it's a positive thing we should see and hear all the time in our lives. Our lives will be far more fruitful if we have better input from the Bible. Many cry foul to this, too—"Well, not necessarily. It's not always the case. You can draw a line between knowing the Bible and reaching the lost." Well, common sense tells us differently. We know that what we see and hear affects us.

The process of getting the Word of God inside of us changes our hearts and minds. And once it's inside, we gain a new motivation

If we're not connected to him properly, then we don't have his words. And if we don't have his words in us, then the fruitful life will not be ours.

to do what it says. Jesus said, "If you remain in me and my words remain in you, ask whatever you wish, and it will be given you" (John 15:7). Christ's words are what flow from him to us. If we're not connected to him properly, then we don't have his words. And if we don't have his words in us, then the fruitful life will not be ours. Three ways can ensure that we are getting the Word of God to "remain" in us… so that we can have the power he wants us to have. These three "M" words should be easy to remember:

MEDITATING THE SCRIPTURE

Meditating on the Word is one of the most common concepts in the Bible, and it's the fourth spiritual discipline. And it's directly related to fruit. Psalm 1:2 speaks of a delight for God's Word and meditating on it "day and night." So this sounds great. How do we meditate, then? Sometimes when we hear the word "meditate" we think of an Eastern man sitting in an uncomfortable position and saying "Ummmm" to himself with his hands held a funny way. That's not the kind of meditation the Scripture teaches. Biblical meditation is not removing all thought from our minds—as much Eastern religion teaches. Biblical meditation focuses on something, not on nothing.

Meditating has three components. First, meditation means thinking about it. Just think about it. Sit down and read or discuss the Bible. Think about a particular passage or truth for five minutes in the shower. Think about what it might mean generally. Think about what it might mean for you. You don't have to be a scholar to think about the Bible. In fact, your thinking about the Bible may be less cloudy than the scholars!

Second, meditation means focusing on it. When you focus on Scripture, you don't skim it. You wouldn't "meditate" on the book of 2 Kings. There's just too much there. You might, however, focus on 2 Kings 2:9b, where Elisha says to his mentor Elijah, "Let me inherit a double portion of your spirit." I've meditated on that verse more than any other verse in the Bible. It comes to mind all the time because I've focused on it so narrowly. It's a concept that captivates my imagination. God speaks to me as I focus on that verse. Actually, it's half of a verse. That's okay. In order to meditate you must focus. (Does that make you think about Mr. Miagi in Karate Kid saying "must focus"? It does me. But that just shows that I may have meditated on lines from 1980s movies as much as I have on many parts of Scripture.)

Third, meditation means listening to it. Just listen. Read a very short passage and then listen to God. That's meditation. Take out a notepad and write down what you think God might be saying. Don't run out ahead of yourself and try to apply or "get out of the verse" something too quickly. Don't preemptively do the Holy Spirit's job. Don't think of what "others" need to hear about it. That's communication—not meditation (something I'm tempted to do more than most, I fear.) Why do you think Jesus said so often, "He who has ears to hear, let him hear" (Mark 4:9,23). Have ears to hear when you meditate.

MEMORIZING THE SCRIPTURE

Part of the reason memorizing is so hard for many is that you haven't meditated on what you want to memorize. So don't try to memorize until after you've meditated for some time. Also, try to memorize what those verses that God has spoken to you from, since it will be all the more personal and meaningful. Your motivation will burn hotter for this reason.

You haven't meditated on what you want to memorize.

Maybe another reason memorizing seems so hard is that you treat it like memorizing in school. You use a "cram for the test" method of memorization. My mother always told me that I was just putting those studies into my "short term memory" when I did that. She was right. I can't tell you the first thing about algebra or Spanish—but I think I aced a lot of tests in both.

Memorizing scripture is long-term memorization. Instead of hoping to memorize huge portions of scripture—just try one. Stick with it till you have it. Review it. Pull it out every day or every other day. Even after you've moved on to memorizing something else, keep going back to the beginning and review—seeing if it's long-term memory. You need to find your own pace for memorization and build from there. Don't use someone else's timetable. Respond to your own and the Spirit.

However, make sure you use someone else's method. Hundreds of wonderful Bible memorization methods exist—and if you actually implement most any of them, you'll have a system to keep you on task and keep you accountable.

MEDIATING THE SCRIPTURE

You're a mediator for those who don't know Christ around you.

Once you've meditated on the portions of Scripture that mean the most to you, and committed them to memory… then it's time to pass them on. Mediating the Scripture means communicating it. Mediating is "going between" two things. A "mediator" is someone who negotiates between two individuals. A "media" in the

Memorization Tips from
Dennis Jackson:

- Read the passage several times
- Read it out loud
- Write it down and review it
- Personalize it
- Have a memorization partner
- Review it weekly

technical sense is something that filters and transmits the most important information or material.

You're a mediator for those who don't know Christ around you. They haven't memorized Scripture. They haven't meditated on it day and night. If you have then you get the opportunity to pass on some of what they are missing. So often you struggle with what to say to someone who isn't in relationship with Jesus Christ. What God would have you do is mediate what he would say to them. You can put it in your own words, for sure, but pass it on. Then you don't have to do all the thinking. Let God figure it out. The Bible says of itself, "My word...shall not return to me void" (Isaiah 55:11). When you consider the evangelistic fruit of your life, and it seems void of it, then determine to use more of the Word according to this promise. Start small with meditation... then memorizing in bits and pieces... then mediating the Scripture to those who need it most will come naturally to you.

Day 33

Secret Service

When no one is looking, do you serve others or serve yourself?

We live with the televangelism curse. This curse works its way between our motivation to see people come to Christ and our actions and effectiveness in doing so. The televangelism curse is a product of the general hypocrisy that has been suspected and often proven to exist in the evangelists on television. Whether because of the few televangelists who have actually turned out to have impure intentions and unholy lifestyles or because of a media intent on making a mountain out of those molehills—the televangelism curse has ensured that the unfortunate taint of hypocrisy stains all things evangelistic.

We feel it in our hearts when we consider sharing our faith with someone who does not yet know Christ. Something inside us says, "I don't want to say anything because they'll think I'm some sort of Bible-freak, and then my life will be under a microscope from now on." We may even see some hypocrisy in our own lives and that makes us think, "I'm already not living it like I should—I'll get my own act in gear before I share my faith." And in general we're all fearful that we're working uphill when we share our faith. It's as though the culture around us already thinks Christians are hypocritical Bible-thumpers who will tell them they're going to hell, then ask for money.

But there's a simple cure for the televangelism curse. The servant evangelism cure.

These thoughts are all a part of the televangelism curse.

THE SERVANT EVANGELISM CURE

But there's a simple cure for the televangelism curse. The servant evangelism cure. Serving others is our fifth spiritual discipline and has a distinct diffusing nature. When we serve someone we counteract all the bad effects of hypocrisy and judgmentalism. A servant is the least hypocritical person in the world. Hypocrisy is the act of making ourselves look better than others when in fact we're not. Servanthood is the act of making ourselves lower than others when in fact our character is golden. Christians are seen as hypocrites because not enough of us are servants. People may not believe Jesus is the Son of God. They may disagree with his teachings or persecute his people. They may even oppose his way of life. But one thing they never do: they never call him a hypocrite. And that's because he was a servant.

Being a servant to those who don't know Christ also counteracts the reputation Christians have for judgmentalism. A servant is the least judgmental person in the world. Judgmental people point out the flaws in others and condemn them for it. Servanthood is the act of seeing the needs of others and meeting them. Again, Christians are seen as judgmental because not enough of us are servants. In a striking difference between what you'd expect and what he was actually like—Jesus, who was absolutely perfect, came to serve people not judge people. The New Testament is a bold insertion of a non-judgmental but perfect person into an imperfect and naturally judgmental world.

The world may think that becoming a Christian makes one more judgmental. In fact, it should do the opposite. Jesus told us to remove the plank from our own eyes before pointing out the specks in other people's eyes (Matthew 7:3-5).

TRULY SECRET SERVICE

We can serve people a million and one different ways. But more often than not, servanthood has to do with our attitude as much as our actions. One of the best ways to ensure pure servanthood is to do our acts of service in secret. We should be like the secret service agents that guard the President of the United States—no one should notice us. We should blend in with the background when we serve. Often we see the suit and sun-glasses-wearing guards of the president and assume those are the only secret service agents around him. In fact, many agents under cover in plain clothes mingle in the crowds and surround the president at all times. Unfortunately, when we serve we'd rather dress up and look cool and have some kind of identification, like the cords running from the ear of the bodyguards down into their suits. We wouldn't mind being noticed for our service.

We think that in order to produce fruit for God we need to be noticed for what we're doing. But the Bible tells us fruit

It's a test of your trust in God to cover your servanthood tracks.

IN YOUR WORKPLACE
- Remake that pot of coffee when it's low but don't announce that you did it
- Clean up the restroom so it's spotless
- Anonymously drop off candy or snacks in other people's cubicles or stations
- Help someone else finish their work when you're ahead
- Replace the paper or ink in the printer
- Do your work for your boss with a servant's attitude, ready to go the extra mile for him or her

IN YOUR CHURCH
- Drop by the church some Saturday and treat its landscaping even better than your own
- When you hear someone lost their job, drop off some cash at their doorstep or in their mailbox
- Bring groceries and meals over for someone who had a baby or surgery
- Invite every new person you see over to your home and serve them a nice dinner
- Find out what your pastor can't seem to get done and offer to do it for him or her
- Ask what ministry is in greatest need of help in the church and volunteer there for a year—just helping out with the simplest tasks

IN YOUR SMALL GROUP
- Have the group in your home
- Bring snacks and then make people take them home with them
- When you hear of a need in the group meet that need in secret

- Serve them by praying daily for their needs
- Do things for them you would normally do only for a family member

IN YOUR GROUP OF FRIENDS
- Don't just chat with them—find out their needs and meet them
- Go the extra mile to do helpful things for them
- Buy them a present you know they want but their family can't afford, and give it to them anonymously
- When you hear of a big project they're doing on a certain day—show up at their house that day and give unexpected help

happens even when no one ever finds out. Don't plant "service grenades," acts of kindness that you have orchestrated to "go off" at a certain time so that you'll get the credit. Practice the discipline of not only serving, but covering the tracks of your service. When doing some secret act of service and the thought comes to you—"I wonder if anyone sees me doing this?"—don't dwell on it and hope someone will notice. Instead, figure out a way to make sure no one notices. Then look to God and say, "It's okay if no one ever knows this, God, because I'm ultimately doing it for you."

It's a test of your trust in God to cover your servanthood tracks. And God finds a way to not only use your service to point to him, but also to honor you in the end. You will receive your reward in heaven—the true "in the end" of life.

The Fruitful Life

GOING DEEPER

If you're now turned on to the idea of servant evangelism read Steve Sjogren's wonderful book

Conspiracy of Kindness: A Refreshing New Approach to Sharing the Love of Jesus with Others. Ann Arbor, MI: Servant Publications © 1993.

Receiving and Giving Coaching

You are competent to instruct one another.

That phrase is not mine. The Apostle Paul said this in the book of Romans (15:14). It's a significant phrase. Paul is not just saying the Romans are generally competent people. He's saying they are competent enough to "instruct" each other. When you think of the word "instructor" you often think of experts in some field, teaching what they know. When you think of parachuting instructors, you expect that they have been parachuting before. When you hear of driving instructors, you'd expect them to have their driver's licenses and know a thing or two more about driving than the average person. When you see scuba diving instructors, you expect that they have been underwater more than you have.

But this is not true of the people Paul said should "instruct." Not only were they just average people with ordinary resumes, Paul didn't even know what these people were like in the first place. You see, Paul had not even met these people. He had not yet been to the Roman church. Other people started it. So how did he know they were competent to do anything? They could have been a bunch of chuckleheads for all he knew.

In fact, many of the Roman converts were likely former slaves and very poor. Many were likely women, who in that culture had much less education and leadership skills than women in our world. Why would Paul say they were competent? He must have known something most people didn't.

The only qualification that matters is whether you know Christ.

THE ONLY QUALIFICATON THAT MATTERS

Something resides inside all Christians that makes them competent to instruct other disciples: the Holy Spirit. This competence is the fifth spiritual discipline. The only qualification that matters is whether you know Christ. If you know Christ, he's given you his Spirit. His Spirit works through you to make you competent to instruct other people.

The Spirit speaks through broken vessels. He speaks through you from time to time, and are you perfect? Well then, it's no big leap to presume that other imperfect disciples around you may be spoken through from time to time, too, even with their rough edges thrown in. Think of instructing as coaching. Everyone needs a little coaching from time to time. And Paul thinks you're competent to do it, because we, like the Romans, have the Holy Spirit in our lives.

When you don't give coaching to other believers, you withhold what the Spirit may want to say through you. And when you don't receive the coaching of other believers, you are inferring that they don't have the Spirit either. Or that you're not interested in what the Holy Spirit wants to teach you through them. Not a great position for a Christian to be in, to say the least.

THE DIFFERENCE COACHING CAN MAKE

Sometimes all it takes to go to the next level is a little coaching. I remember going to a youth camp when I was just 19 years old. I was playing basketball with a bunch of the high school boys. At a break in the game a few of them were trying to dunk the ball. One of the boys, a tall, thin and lanky kid, could "grab the rim" with both hands and could leap super high. But though he tried several times to dunk, like the rest of them, he couldn't do it. I took him aside and told him he could probably dunk by doing just a few things differently. I explained that he needed to take off for his jump a little sooner and he needed to pump the ball with his arms, using his upper body to take off just as much as his legs. After a few more tries, he dunked the ball for the first time in front of his friends. After the cheers and high-fives, he went around again and dunked. Then again, and again, and again. With just ten minutes of coaching he went from *almost* to *every time.* That's the difference coaching can make.

> *They need your brief moment of coaching to go to the next level. Don't withhold from them the slam-dunk experience that could result from your simple tips.*

So many people are almost where they want to be as believers. But they need your brief moment of coaching to go to the next level. Don't withhold from them the slam-dunk experience that could result from your simple tips.

BECOMING A COACHABLE PERSON

More often than not people would rather give coaching than receive it. Dishing it out becomes second nature, but taking it hardly ever feels truly natural. But some people learn over time to become coachable people. In sports, it's an attitude that teams and coaches look for. Instead of just talent, they want someone who is coachable. Here are several ways to become a coachable person:

•   Be on the lookout for a different perspective—part of being coachable is learning to appreciate that you don't see everything. Your perspective is limited. Look out for those people who can give you a different perspective on who you are and what you do.

•   Welcome criticism—you're hard-wired to run from criticism. But after reaching a certain level of confidence in who you are, you can begin to actually receive and even welcome criticism. When you get to this point and someone well-meaning and helpful offers coaching, you welcome it like icing on the cake.

•   Capture the key issues and mirror them back—one way to receive coaching from someone else is to boil down what they are saying and repeat the issues back to them. This helps you capture the most important things in what they are saying, drop the parts that might offend you or make you question yourself, and then inspire confidence in the person coaching you, letting them know that you actually get what they're trying to tell you.

•   Thank people for coaching you—this honest thank-you can help that person know that your door is always open for well-meant coaching. When you thank them for it, you also admit to them and yourself that you needed it—which you did.

•   Feed back the application of the coaching—after following through on the coaching advice, tell the coach how it went. Process additional comments on how it went, and ask for more tweaks or advice on the original thought. The most coachable people are great at this!

•   Divide the harmful from the helpful—sometimes the coaching you receive goes too far and discourages you. It's important to separate any and all of the harmful things said from the helpful things. Some people are just more harmful than anything else to you—and they are the ones you can just stop listening to all together. Coachable people are sensitive enough to coaching that they know they can't listen to hurtful people or it would scar them deeply.

BECOMING A HELPFUL COACH

It's important to be coachable before you go on to coaching others. So follow the above steps first. Then you'll know how it feels to be coached. I think that's why many of the best coaches in sports used to be average or even mediocre athletes themselves. They know what it's like to be coached to the next level. Then they become great at coaching in a helpful way.

• You can't give it till you can take it—nobody wants to be instructed by a perfectionist. Paul was on to something when he wrote the Romans—instruction often comes best from peers. If you can take coaching, then you become the perfect person to pass on what you've learned. If you can't take it, then you end up not having learned enough to pass on anyway.

• Realize that coaching should never be one way—when you head into that other person's office or call them up or pull them aside after church, walk into that situation open to allowing them to coach you back. If you think they're the only ones who need to learn something, then you've got a lot to learn. The best coaches often start out their coaching by saying, "I've noticed this thing about you lately…can you help me understand that?" Sometimes that understanding is actually all that's needed—not the coaching.

• Encouraging someone over time gives you the platform to coach—this applies in two ways: 1) you need to be an overall believer and encourager to the people you want to coach and 2) you need to start your conversation by encouraging them. Offer them an "encouragement sandwich" when you coach. Start with a short, encouraging statement of your belief in them, offer the coaching, then repeat something reassuring about their ability to go to the next level.

• Ensure your coaching flows from the Word—Colossians 3:16a says, "Let the word of Christ dwell in you richly as you teach and admonish one another with all wisdom." Your coaching isn't just your random opinions. It's the word of Christ flowing through you. Admonishment is a lost art in today's church. Often it's not because we aren't willing to offer our opinion, people do that all the time. Usually it's because the word of Christ isn't dwelling in us enough for us to offer true and effective admonishment.

•　　　Walk the tact balance beam—be tactful in your coaching. Tact is the balance beam between not saying enough for them to get the point and saying too much so that they are offended. Walk down the middle.

•　　　Sometimes it's a risk to coach—you can't be sure how your coaching will be received. It's always a risk to step out and offer a few coaching tips to someone. It takes guts to do this, but nobody grows without it.

•　　　Develop a community that coaches—cultures that coach one another gain great benefits. People who are uncoachable are magnets for other uncoachable people. The reverse is also true: the more coachable you are, the more coachable those you associate with will be. You reproduce in like kind. Or worse, you become a hybrid disciple, like a seedless watermelon that can't reproduce and has no fruit at all.

Day 35

Relationships

Your relationships will be the toughest part.

It takes even more spiritual discipline to have good relationships, which is the sixth spiritual discipline, than to have a deep devotional life. It will take way more elbow grease to resolve a conflict with a friend than to memorize three chapters of Scripture.

Consider these relational truths:

- Every marriage is perfect, until after the honeymoon.
- Every family is perfect, until the children are born.
- Every small group is perfect, until the people show up.
- Every church is perfect, until they open the doors on Sunday.

WHAT'S YOUR EMOTIONAL QUOTIENT?

Every person starts at a different place on the emotional quotient chart. This EQ is the level of relational ability you have. It's how well you interact with people, how effectively you build friendships, how you read a room, how you communicate, and how you listen. Your EQ is a way to help you see where you're at when it comes to relationships.

Just like it is with IQ (intelligence quotient), some people have more to work with from the start when it comes to relational abilities. Fortunately, many with a lower IQ have a very high EQ! This may even be why your dog is a better friend to you than the geniuses you know. Genius = high IQ, low EQ. Dog = no IQ, high EQ.

GOING DEEPER

For a very practical overview of ten spiritual disciplines read John Ortberg's book

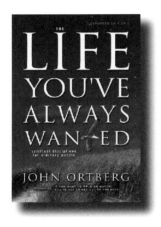

The Life You've Always Wanted: Spiritual Disciplines for Ordinary People. Grand Rapids, MI: Zondervan © 2002.

For some reason God seems to create people with one of these assets much higher than the other. Most people with above average intelligence have relational struggles. And most people who are just incredible with people and are the life of the party feel like they aren't as smart as the quiet ones in the corner. It's not always true—but nearly always seems to be the case.

SOMETHING TO WORK WITH

But even those with a lower EQ have something to work with. It's like people whose IQ isn't high enough to become college professors, but they are smart enough to do a certain job—or to teach their kids. Your relational EQ is high enough to get you somewhere.

And remember, in your weakness he is strong. Many dyslexic people are the most successful academics in their field. Once they identify their learning style, they become more intentional about the way they read and learn and by doing so begin to learn better than anyone around them.

If you have a lower EQ, then you can do the same. Remember first that you're not alone. Many people struggle relationally. It's nothing to be ashamed of. You may just not be wired up like that life of the party. No big deal. If you struggle with building relationships, then map out exactly why you do what you do—or don't do what you'd like to do. What are your specific issues? Then become more intentional about the way you interact with people and build friendships. By doing so you will begin to be more effective than even those for whom relationships come naturally. People with a high EQ often don't think about relationships—because they don't have to. But it also makes them miss things from time to time. If you're intentional about relationships, you might just be better in the end than they are. Anyway, you've probably got that whole IQ thing going for you.

RELATIONAL EVANGELISM

When it comes to evangelism you've probably been told that you should be "relational." This is a recent code-word we pastors use to infer that we're not asking you to go door to door and blast people with spiritual questions cold-turkey anymore. Aren't you glad?

But you still struggle with what to do when you're asked to do "relational evangelism." The problem you may have with relational evangelism is not just the evangelism part—but the relational part. Many of you just aren't that relational, and you have to be intentional, as you've seen above. But further—many of you just don't have a very large part of your life devoted to being relational with people who don't yet know Christ. You may know some people you'd like to befriend that are unchurched, but you just don't know how to start.

DIFFERENT WAYS TO GET STARTED

Every Christian is unique, right? The church is full of different people! Why wouldn't this also be true about people that aren't Christians? They're different, too! So don't think that the same simple plan is going to work in reaching all these different people for Jesus. Look at people as individuals. There are several ways to get started with that person at work or in your neighborhood with whom you want to build an authentic redemptive relationship.

Your friend may think church is the dullest place on earth. Change that perception by doing something together that interests him or her. Get involved in something they're already doing or talking of doing. But do it together and do it just for fun. You need more fun in your life anyway. By starting with something that truly interests them, it's hard for them not to want to spend time with you. And time is crucial with building relationships. Get started with something that interests your friend.

Your friend may not need you to beat around the bush. I bet you hate it when you get that telemarketing call where the caller won't get to the point. The marketer asks random questions that don't have anything to do with the bottom line. Same thing here. Sometimes you need to cut to the chase with your friend and inspire them with how excited you are. Don't soft sell it—just cut loose on how important your spiritual life is for you. It will inspire them to have that same kind of excitement in their lives. With some friends you can just jump right in and get them excited about spiritual relationships. So get started by inspiring your friend.

Your friend may not want to take it all "hook, line and sinker" without checking things out for a while. So give them that opportunity. Include them in church! More than inviting them to services, including them is about community. In fact, you may want your friend to come to your small group or a fun outing with other Christians long before you invite him or her to a service. Get started by including your friend in your church life.

Your friend may have a lot of issues. Don't we all? You may not see yourself as having many answers—but if your friend knows you at all they may see something in you they want to learn from. They're not looking to upset the apple cart of their lives too much yet. But their cart has enough rotten apples that they are ready to learn from you. It might be time to try investing in your friend. Invest extended time. Invest authentic advice. Invest some compassion for their situation. You may be the closest thing they have to a Christlike influence. So get started by investing in your friend.

Your friend may be ripe for an invitation. Sometimes people are just waiting for someone to invite them. You may be the one to extend it. The invite can be a big one—like coming to a church service with you. Or it can be a small invite—like joining you for a fun event at the church or with your small group. Just do it! Get started by simply inviting your friend.

Your friend may look busy all the time. People run from meeting to meeting at work. They may only go outside to wash their cars. They may be chasing after kids constantly. But many times people are just trying to look busy. Sometimes you have to actually interrupt in order to build a relationship. It may just be a two-minute interruption so you can offer to help them with their work, or washing their car, or with the kids. Get started by interrupting them if you have to.

Your friend may have a lot to offer. Sometimes people don't get interested in church or spiritual things because they don't know what it has to offer them. Well, turn the tables on them. Instead of starting with all you've got to give them, start with all they've got to give to the church. Not money—but what they're good at. Involve them in a ministry. Hundreds of ways exist to serve in church. Nearly anyone can help. But do that ministry together—so you can get to know your friend better while doing it. Get started by involving your friend in serving.

There are so many ways to get started with your friend. Choose one of these ways or come up with your own, something tailor-made for building a truly redemptive, authentic relationship. But whatever you choose to do, get started right away.

Week Five
29.30.31.32.33.34.35.
Group Questions

1)   What annoying habits do you have that you wish you could stop doing? What annoying habits do other people have that you wish they would stop doing?

2)   Without peeking, recall as a group this week's seven disciplines that result in fruit:
    i)
    ii)
    iii)
    iv)
    v)
    vi)
    vii)

3)   What are some other spiritual disciplines that you think may help people produce eternal fruit?

The Fruit of the Disciplines   155

4)   Report your "My Five" list to the group (page 124). Then pray over all the names as a group. Pair up people to pray in an ongoing way for each other's lists.

5)   Share what has worked and what hasn't worked for those in your group when it comes to fasting.

6)   Do any of the six dimensions of the confessional life not make sense to you? Discuss them in the group. How might your group do a better job at confession together?

7)   Brainstorm in your group about some secret service ideas for reaching non-Christians. Make plans to implement together at least one of your ideas.

the fruit of multiplication

There's more to life than simple addition. In fact, adding things to our lives is part of our problem. We add so much to life that we can't keep up. We add this and add that. Halfway through the day we realize that it just doesn't all add up. Instead, we can lead lives of multiplication. When it comes to living a fruitful life the really amazing fruit comes when you harness the power of multiplication. By multiplying fruit you grow the Kingdom of God without adding anything at all to your own life. Multiplication is the best way to do more with less.

Week Six Memory Verse:

You did not choose me, but I chose you and appointed you to go and bear fruit --fruit that will last. Then the Father will give you whatever you ask in my name. – John 15:16

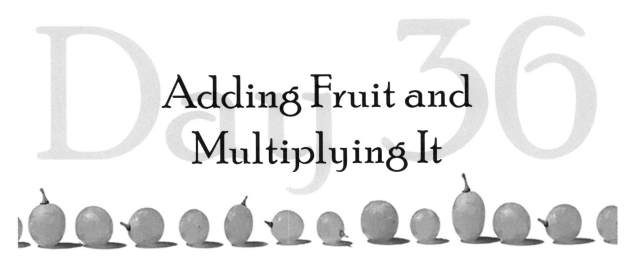

Adding Fruit and Multiplying It

God wants you to multiply what he's given you.

If you are connected in the vine, God will add fruit to your life. If the conditions are right, fruit is a natural and expected thing. If you believe and apply the previous five weeks of concepts, the fruitful life will eventually be automatic for you. But it doesn't stop there.

Here's a little math test for you:

$4 + 4 =$ _____

$4 \times 4 =$ _____

Which is better?

Even an elementary school child will take the bigger number. Bigger is better. Well, you might say, if it's four pimples times four junk e-mails, then I'll take the lesser one. But what if the four things are good things? You'd always choose the bigger number. More of a good thing is always a good thing. When it comes to good results, less is never more.

THE BEST THING

Life offers many good things. But we've spent five weeks talking about the best thing: fruit. What will you be remembered for? How much fruit you produced in the vine for Christ. If more of a good thing is always a good thing then more of the best thing is the best thing. That's where multiplication comes in.

When the early church was meeting house to house in small groups and in the temple courts as a larger group, they were doing all sorts of things that produced fruit (Acts 2:42-47). They were devoted to the teaching of the Word. They lived in constant fellowship and hospitality. They broke bread in communion with one another. And they prayed continually. Sound familiar? They are the same things we have just studied, things that produce a fruitful life. But perhaps the most important thing they did that relates to us is their multiplication. They didn't just do a lot of good things and keep to themselves. They multiplied.

GOD REAPS WHERE HE DOES NOT SOW

Matthew 25 records the parable of the talents. Jesus told a fascinating story about the nature of our Father in heaven. The story goes like this: A wealthy man was going on a long business trip. He called three of his servants in and gave five gold bars called "talents" to one of them, two to another and just one to a third. Then he left.

The man with five talents immediately put his to work and doubled his money to ten. The man with two talents did the same and ended with four. But the man with just one talent went and buried it in the ground.

A long time later the wealthy master came home and called his servants to him. The first two men showed up with double the master's money. The master replied with the same statement to both of these servants: "Well done, good and faithful servant! You have been faithful with a few things; I will put you in charge of many things. Come and share your master's happiness!"

But the man who received one talent came before the master and said, "Master, I knew that you are a hard man, harvesting where you have not sown and gathering where you have not scattered seed. So I was afraid and went out and hid your talent in the ground. See, here is what belongs to you."

The master was livid! He called him "wicked" and "lazy" and confirmed that he was the kind of master who reaped where he didn't sow and gathered where he didn't plant seeds. He took the man's one talent, gave it to the one with ten, then tossed the good-for-nothing servant out "into the darkness, where there will be weeping and gnashing of teeth."

Note these factors related to multiplication from this story:

1) Whatever you're given you're expected to multiply it
2) Simply holding onto what you've got doesn't cut it
3) God expects returns through you in places he hasn't even personally planted seeds
4) The place the servants who multiplied went to obviously refers to heaven
5) The place the servant who didn't multiply was tossed into obviously refers to hell

God reaps where he does not sow. He gathers people into his fold because of multiplication. He counts on you to do this while he's away on "business."

EXPONENTIAL POTENTIAL

So, what are the things that multiply your fruit rather than simply adding to it? I've thought long and hard about this question. It's a tough call. You can spend your life doing so many good things. Many noble and God-honoring activities are fruitful. But the question we're asking now is not just what is fruitful—we're now asking what multiplies fruit.

I believe four actions have the potential to multiply your kingdom fruit exponentially. By this I mean expressly spiritual things. Plenty of worldly things can be multiplied. Rabbits and the stock market are the first ones that come to my mind. But what multiplies spiritual things? What multiplies eternal fruit? And by this I mean truly multiplying—as in more than simply adding fruit to your life. These four actions are inherently multiplication oriented. In fact, they multiply your fruit exponentially. These four actions eventually leave your control and multiply all by themselves. This is the key to multiplication. Once you multiply a multiplier it becomes exponential. In mathematics, which was always the lowest grade on my report card, I learned that when a number like this[10] appears at the end of something that means it is multiplied that many times against itself. For instance, 10 x 10 = 100. But, 10^{10} = 100,000,000,000. It is math shorthand for exponential multiplying.

FOUR FRUIT MUTIPLIERS

Each of these four fruit multipliers has exponential power for your life. For that reason I've added that little to-the-tenth-power number behind them in each chapter. I also reveal the exponential potential of each of these multipliers in each chapter. It should help you be more intentional about the multiplication factor in your own fruitful life.

Four actions have the potential to multiply your kingdom fruit exponentially

The Fruitful Life

The four things that have the potential to exponentially multiply your kingdom fruit are:

Multiplying Disciples in Your Family[10]
Multiplying Mentors[10]
Multiplying Community[10]
Multiplying Churches[10]

Your spiritual passion might not show up directly in the titles of these four things. However, in the next four days, try to see the connection between what you're most passionate about and how it may fit into the broader spectrum of these four fruit multipliers. God may have given you that passion for the express purpose of multiplying kingdom fruit. Because that is his top priority.

What will you be remembered for? How much fruit you produced in the vine for Christ

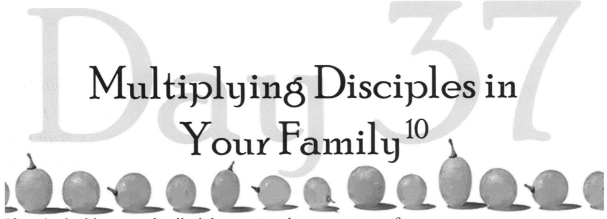

Multiplying Disciples in Your Family[10]

If you're looking to make disciples, start under your own roof.

No domain is more painfully slow to produce fruit than the family. But no riper an opportunity exists to deeply develop disciples of Jesus Christ than in your family. The family is often a place of complexities too thick for outsiders to understand. But it is also the incubator for nearly every person's future. Believers today have mostly forgotten the power of a family in making and multiplying disciples.

THE FORGOTTEN FRUIT OF FAMILY

The central spiritual unit of faith for the Jews of Jesus' day was the family. This is partly what made the religion of Judaism and then Christianity such portable religions. Nearly all other religions were so focused on "place" that they lost everything when moved around. However, Judaism was nearly always a religion on the move, and therefore centered in the moving family. And even more so Christianity has almost never been a place with a "hometown." Rather, the family has been its "home." The church has largely lost this central role of family in the life of faith. Recapturing that dynamic is the key to multiplication.

Believers today have mostly forgotten the power of a family in making and multiplying disciples.

BE FRUITFUL AND MULTIPLY

God's first command to Adam and Eve was simple, "Be fruitful and multiply." Their to-do list was pretty elementary back there in the Garden of Eden! From the very beginning God's primary plan for you was to have children and teach them to know and follow him. Many today don't take that command seriously enough. They outsource the responsibility to make disciples of their children to their churches. They need to gain back that primary responsibility and take ownership of that role. You don't have to be Bible scholars to disciple your children. That's the great thing about children. They have no clue that you don't really know that much. Children are your very best opportunity to make disciples. Start there.

That's the great thing about children: they have no clue that you don't really know that much.

MAKING A DISCIPLE OUT OF YOUR SPOUSE

Every marriage is a work in progress. Perhaps you have become a disciple but your spouse is either not yet a follower of Christ or is just beginning. Don't worry—someone had to go first. It just happened to be you. That may be a part of God's plan. You accepted his grace first or began to get serious about following him first. So now it's your role to have the patience to let your spouse catch up while being intentional in making a disciple out of him or her. Here's how to pull off this little dance with your spouse:

1)   Don't guilt them into it. That's not going to work. They need to become a true disciple (follower of Jesus) for the right reasons. Double-check the things you do that might make them feel too guilt-ridden to actually respond. The best thing to do is be honest and actually ask them: "I want to encourage you in your spiritual life, but am I doing anything that's making you feel guilty rather than encouraged?"

2)   Your actions speak louder than your words. The way you follow Jesus will rub off on your spouse more than your speeches about what they should be doing. Remember the plank in your own eye, and don't start judging the specks in your spouse's eye (Matthew 7:3-5). Saint Francis of Assisi said something once that you ought to think on frequently: "Preach the gospel at all times—if necessary use words."

3)   Let them go at their own pace—but don't let up. Be consistent and don't let them drift off. It may get frustrating when you're growing so much faster than they are, but they may have a different pace than you do.

4)   Start growing together. Do a study together—of any kind. Ask questions about the way your spouse is growing already. Cheer on the little steps. But pace yourself enough to grow with them instead of around them.

5)   Put the ball in your spouse's court. Ask them what they think their next step is spiritually. Wonder aloud with them about when they think they'll be ready to follow Jesus fully. Ultimately, their decision is not your responsibility, but it would mean the world for you if they got fired up about their faith.

6)   Get other people involved. They may just need to hear it all from another perspective. Get your spouse in the same room with other Christians you trust. Make your Christian friends your spouse's friends too. Don't live a double life. Include your spouse in your life with Christ.

Multiplying Mentors[10]

You haven't fulfilled your role till you've filled your shoes.

What will you be remembered for? You've been asking that question over and over again in this journey. Today, consider what you shouldn't be remembered for. When you are gone, those left behind shouldn't say, "Those will be hard shoes to fill." That kind of legacy makes you feel great about yourself, but it is short lived. Far better for them to say, "He [or she] left big shoes to fill, but his successor is poised to take us to the next level."

SUCCESSFUL SUCCESSORS

Many people have been effective and successful in history—but those who have had the most lasting impact have been those who established a successor to take over for them. Successors are raised up in multiple ways. Sometimes they are hand-picked. Other times they are biological (sons and daughters). Many times they are completely random. But if you want to truly multiply the kingdom, then you need to think about who comes after you as much as you think about what you're doing today.

Think about who comes after you as much as you think about what you're doing today.

Elijah was one of the greatest mentors ever as he picked Elisha to be his successor. At the end of Elijah's life, Elisha asked for a double portion of Elijah's spirit. In a fascinating answer to that request, Elisha ended up doing twice as many miracles as Elijah.

John the Baptist understood what it meant to multiply through a successor. When he had the attention of the people and even the king, he knew he needed to step aside for his cousin Jesus. That's when he spoke these famous words: "He must become greater; I must become

The Fruitful Life

less" (John 3:30). That's the ultimate motto for those who want to multiply the kingdom even after they are gone.

Two early church saints are a good example of hand-picking a successor. St. Ambrose built a relationship with St. Augustine (long before he was a saint and was still quite a sinner). Augustine showed up one day while Ambrose was preaching. Ambrose walked down into the crowd, dragged Augustine to the altar in the front and practically forced him to accept Christ and change his ways. Not long after Augustine became a more worthy successor to Ambrose and far outshone his influence.

Two presidents of the United States understood what it meant to raise up generational successors. Founding Father John Adams and recent president George H. W. Bush were both defeated after their first terms in office. However, both men raised sons that were later elected to be presidents! Imagine that. Both men got the last laugh against their opponents. Even when they lost, they saw their sons pick up the torch after them.

In Spring Lake Wesleyan Church, we have personally experienced an amazing story of succession. Ralph Baynum was our pastor for 22 years, an extremely long time in this day and age. Because of the great succession relationship between Pastor Ralph and Pastor Dennis Jackson, our church experienced seamless growth and transition. Many churches would have plateaued or even faltered after such a long-tenured pastor left. But Pastor Ralph showed he cared more about multiplying the kingdom than patting his own back on the way out.

MULTIPLYING YOUR TIME TO MENTOR

Perhaps you think your life is too full to mentor other people. Or maybe you think you have little to offer. Gain some motivation to make the time by reminding yourself that you won't be remembered as much for what you did as for who you invested in. And gain motivation by starting with just a few close companions. Jesus modeled that principle for you.

The pattern of Jesus was to decrease down to a small circle of individuals those he wished to have the most impact on in life. There were thousands of people that came to hear him tell stories, answer critics, and perform miracles. More than a hundred people were his close followers. Twelve of those were hand-picked as disciples. Then three of those were his inner circle. Jesus knew he needed to multiply his time to mentor by focusing his efforts on a few.

If you are married or have children, these people must be in your inner circle, no matter what kind of a relationship you have with them. This was the focus of the prior chapter. But you may also have a few other non-family members in your inner circle. If you are single, like Jesus, you have the opportunity to choose all those you mentor, even your innermost circle.

You'll be remembered for who came after you and filled your shoes

What will you be remembered for? I hope you'll be remembered for who came after you and filled your shoes.

Multiplying Community[10]

A narrow definition of what a small group is can hamper the community of a church

The ultimate power of a group is its potential for growth and multiplication.

A good amount of confusion exists about small groups in church life. Two main problems continue: churches often have too narrow a definition of what a small group is, and church people think small groups might be a fad in church programming that will pass with time.

A narrow definition of what a small group is can hamper the community of a church. And community is what it's all about. "Fellowship" might be the word you would use. Small groups are not a narrow program of the church. The church will always function best when smaller groups of people are getting together. In fact, I would question whether an organization with a huge crowd but no one ever getting together in some kind of smaller groups is really a church at all. It would be more like a rally for people of similar tastes. Not the body of Christ. Smaller groups in the church are not a fad. Even calling them "essential" is an understatement. Without them we wouldn't be who we are in Christ.

GROUPS WITH PURPOSE

But groups are not an end unto themselves. You could note a bunch of benefits and purposes for getting together in groups: studying the Bible, encouragement, worship in song, teaching, service, fun, sharing meals, prayer, sharing, accountability, making disciples, reaching out in community, challenging one anoth-

The most powerful thing is your group's potential for growth and multiplication.

er, supporting each other, loving relationships, etc. These are all the reasons we are inherently drawn to a smaller group of people in church. But for some reason, the most strategic and powerful purpose and benefit of your group may seem less attractive to you than all these things. And that most powerful thing is your group's potential for growth and multiplication.

A church is only as open as its smaller groups. In theory you want your church as a whole to be open to outsiders and newcomers. But when it comes down to opening up your inner circle to outsiders and newcomers, you find you're not too keen on it and you're downright negligent in inviting and including others. The church as a whole becomes ingrown when its smaller groups are ingrown. Instead of biblical community the church becomes an ingrown clique. None of you wants that, I'm sure. But it is accomplished by default when you forget that in the growth of your group lays powerful potential for kingdom fruit.

THE CLOSED DOOR

This is never truer than when it comes to including in your groups those who do not yet know Christ. You often seek out mature Christians that are like you when looking for new people. In fact, the people you should seek out are those brand new Christians or seekers in the church. Or even those people in your workplaces and neighborhoods who might be included in your group before accepting an invitation to services.

At one point in his ministry Jesus went on a long tirade against hypocrisy. In his first rant he says, "How terrible it will be for you teachers of religious law and you Pharisees. Hypocrites! For you won't let others enter the Kingdom of Heaven, and you won't go in yourselves." Matthew 23:13 (NLT).

Jesus calls us out for pretending holiness while being sick inside. It is not the sickness that repulses him. He came, as you might recall, not for the healthy, but the sick (Luke 5:31). It is the pretense of health that he calls out—the claim that there is no sickness within. By doing this, even though we are in a position to know better, we are pulling others down with us. Many "friends" who see through our self-righteous hypocrisy are not only right, but in being unable to resolve that ill-fated excuse; those "friends" walk the path of eternal death unknowingly. This makes our sin all the more distasteful for Jesus. Jesus will ensure that those who pretend to be heaven's gatekeepers will not only close the doors on others but will also themselves be outside of the door to heaven.

THE THREE LEGGED STOOL

Is it hard for you or other members of your group to be motivated to grow and multiply? You like your group just as it is? Then consider this: someone had to invite you in or start a new group in order for you to experience the group you're in. So why should others not get what you've got?

Three ways can effectively ensure that your group isn't shutting the door to heaven for others. Think of them as a balanced three-legged stool for community. If you keep these three practices in mind as a group, then you lock into the strategic power of group life.

• ***Keeping an open chair***—this is a very simple visual exercise that reinforces the idea of openness. Right before prayer time in your group, pull a chair from another room or point out one that is already empty. Then ask everyone to pray for the person that might fill that empty chair. Who could be invited and included in the group? Pray for open hearts to newcomers, and open eyes to those who don't have what your group already takes for granted—community. Use the phrase "open chair" to remind people about this fundamental value in your group. You don't need to be the leader of the group to do this. You just need a heart for those left out.

• ***Developing future leaders***—could you contribute to leading your group? Why not? Are you a potential future leader of your own group? Why not? The most significant barrier to groups growing and multiplying is the lack of leaders. If your group is developing future leaders, then it doesn't put any ceilings on what God could do with your group. You're ready for the future. You're prepared.

• ***Planting new groups***—much like planting a new church, sending out a group of people to start a new small group is a momentous occasion. Treat it as such! Prepare for it months ahead of time by praying about it. Then when the time comes, celebrate it. It's not a sad day—it's a reason to be proud of your group. Only the healthiest groups can plant a new small group with joy. Lay hands on the individuals who are going out to start the new group. Pray for them and commission them for the new work. Then consider that new group your baby and care for its leaders along the way just like a newborn.

From God's perspective, smaller groups are a great thing. But I suspect he sees us missing the strategic benefit of these groups. So often we're satisfied to make the groups all about us instead of all about him. When we do make our groups about glorifying him, we see those on the outside the way he does—and we leave the 99 to go find just one of them.

Multiplying Churches[10]

You are the church, and the church must multiply.

You might wonder what you have to do with multiplying the church. That may seem like an outlandish idea. You're just one person. "How could I multiply churches?" But the catch is that you are the church. The church is not the building you worship in. It's not some idea that you are a part of. It's not a group of people you show up to see. It's you. You're the church.

So if the church should multiply, then you should multiply the church.

WHAT WILL IT TAKE TO REACH YOUR COMMUNITY?

If you have a fruitful life then you want to see your community reached for Jesus. You not only want those in your neighborhood or workplace to come to know Christ—you want everyone to know him. The people at the grocery store, those in the cars on the streets, the masses of neighborhoods all throughout town: you want them all to have what you have in Christ. Every-one!

But how are you going to do that alone? You can't. In your whole lifetime, you couldn't meet everyone in your community. So the church has to do it in one big effort. But even more… how is just your one church going to do that alone? Even if your church had ten services every Sunday, there would still be many that couldn't fit into your building. It's not just about your church—it's about The Church.

All four levels of multiplying fruit work together to reach every single person where you live

The Fruitful Life

All four levels of multiplying fruit work together to reach every single person where you live. Multiplying families, multiplying mentors, multiplying community and multiplying churches all work together to reach those you can't reach alone. Children can reach kids you'll never meet. Those you mentor will reach people long after you're dead. Groups you send out can open up and include people that would never fit with your group. And new churches can reach entire people groups and neighborhoods that your church will barely penetrate. Be a personal encourager and pray about being a personal part of starting new churches in your community. Until the multiplication makes it to that level, many people won't even have a chance to know Christ.

WHAT WILL IT TAKE TO REACH YOUR COUNTRY?

But it's not just about our communities. What about the entire country? Here in the United States many are bemoaning the fact that we are no longer a Christian nation. People are worried that we've left our roots or are betraying our potential for God. Indeed, most countries in the West, including America, could be appropriately termed "Post-Christian." We are seeing a generational decline in church attendance: 54% of our older generations attend church; 49% of the Boomers attend church; and the number drops all the way to just 30% of my own generation, the Busters.[11]

Our country needs a turn-around when it comes to reaching people for Jesus. How will that happen? More churches are the answer. God won't be able to use us much where we don't live. And our church can only do so much. We need more and more fruitful churches to stem the tide that's moving in the opposite direction.

WHAT WILL IT TAKE TO REACH THE WORLD?

In the same light—more churches are needed to reach the world. We shouldn't just send money and prayers around the world, we must send people. And we must send all these things in order to see more churches led by and filled up with people from those countries. On all its levels this adds up to a fruitful multiplication movement that can reach the world.

Is your church an Antioch church or a Jerusalem church?

THE CHOICE: ANTIOCH OR JERUSALEM?

So what can you do about it? How can you help multiply churches? Ask yourself this question: Is your church an Antioch church or a Jerusalem church?

The Jerusalem church described in the book of Acts[12] is a discouraging example of a church not living up to its potential. The Jerusalem church included most of the remaining twelve disciples of Jesus, the great location of the birth of Christianity, and a noble leader in James, the brother of Jesus and the author of the New Testament book bearing his name. However, the church in Jerusalem seemed more concerned with ruling other newly established churches than with multiplying. In nearly every interaction with the Jerusalem church, Paul and the expanding church of the first century found an obstacle. In the most famous passage in Acts 15, Paul and Barnabas go to Jerusalem to solve a big problem. Jewish Christians from the Jerusalem church have been going to Antioch to preach that Gentiles needed to become Jews before they could become Christians. In a strange way, these divisive people were like anti-missionaries. Their actions were slowing down and hindering the movement of the Holy Spirit in the Gentile world, rather than encouraging it.

The Jerusalem Council, as it has come to be known, came to a compromise position after a committee debated the issues. The Jerusalem church does not seem excited about the proposition of Gentiles coming to Christ, but they begrudgingly accept that they can do nothing about it. They pull authority from the anti-missionaries and "allow" the church's expansion. Before the first century concluded, the church in Jerusalem was finished because of persecution and the destruction of the city. The Jerusalem Christians were scattered across the Roman Empire. They were forced because of circumstances to become a sending church. God's will was for that church to multiply, and one way—or another—it did multiply in the end.

The Antioch church was very different from the Jerusalem church. The Antioch church was a diverse group of converts. From the very beginning they preached the Gospel to Gentiles, many of whom accepted Christ. At least one black man (Simeon) and a Cyrene (Lucius) were in the church, as well as Paul and Barnabas, who both taught in the Antioch church. They had a prophet who predicted a famine, and so they immediately sent money to Jerusalem to help the Christians in need there (Acts 11:22-30). And in this town the followers of Jesus first became known as "Christians." We owe our very name to this church.

What's more Acts 13:2-3 records that the people of this church were worshiping the Lord and fasting when the Holy Spirit spoke to them. He told them to set aside Paul (Saul) and Barnabas and send them off to multiply the church. After testing the leading with more fasting and prayer, they did just that.

Imagine sending out missionaries like Paul and Barnabas. Because of the giving and sending nature of this Antioch church, the world never looked the same. They unselfishly sent out their best—and God rewarded the multiplication of the church. Antioch became the basecamp for all the missionary journeys of Paul, and the Roman world was introduced in every corner to Christ.

Surely there were troublesome things happening in Antioch and honorable things happening in the church in Jerusalem. They are not black and white cases of a "good church" and a "bad church." It's not that easy. But likewise, a church can be a "good church" and not be a church that multiplies churches. The churches that existed in Antioch and Jerusalem no longer exist today. In fact, no one church is a permanent entity. "The Church" is, however, permanent. Antioch understood that and became the kind of giving and sending church we should be today. Jerusalem perhaps served another role in God's will—but never seemed to be a giving and sending church. They were more often a receiving and deliberating church.

It took massive persecution for the Jerusalem church to force itself into multiplying itself. Many today worry about a future of persecution in the Western church. If it comes, perhaps God brings it to force us to multiply the church. We are too often a receiving and deliberating church like the church in Jerusalem. May we become a giving and sending church for the glory of God, like the church in Antioch. Then, even after our one specific church is gone—it will live on in the core of many other churches birthed out of it.

Now What?

The Master's Plan for Multiplying Fruit

What is the ultimate fruit of an apple tree?

Is it an apple? That's the obvious answer. It's right in the name, right? But think about it a bit longer. Look at that word "ultimate." That one word changes the question. The first visible fruit of an apple tree may indeed be an apple. But what happens to that apple? It is eaten by someone or something and eventually goes into the ground again. Or it falls to the ground and the apple rots and the seeds are deposited in the ground. Inside that apple-fruit is a more intentional fruit: the seed.

What is your ultimate fruit?

But that seed is not the ultimate fruit, is it? The seed has a purpose—to grow into yet another apple tree. So is the ultimate fruit of an apple tree another apple tree? Close. But not quite.

Does an apple have just one seed? No—it has several. And does an apple tree have just one apple? No—it has hundreds. So each apple tree, when it produces fruit, has the potential to produce many apple trees. And over time, as each generation of trees also produces fruit, the ultimate fruit of just one apple tree is an apple orchard!

So, what is your ultimate fruit? Is it just that one friend whom you would love to see come to Christ? Is it just your children? Is it a handful of neighbors? You have planted seeds in a number of people and will continue to if you live a fruitful life. But they are not the only fruit in your life. They too have seeds they will plant. And those around you in your family, your group, your church, your community, if they are fruitful (and I hope you'll encourage them to be fruitful), will be planting seeds as well. That's how orchards get started. That's how just one fruitful life affects many others.

THE JOHNNY APPLESEED WAY

Have you heard of Johnny Appleseed? Few stories are more sweet and American than that of Johnny Appleseed. Originally John Chapman, the man that became known as "The Apple Man" or "Johnny Appleseed" left Massachusetts to explore the frontier of the northern territory now carved into Michigan, Ohio, Illinois and Indiana. He brought with him the seeds from his orchards in the east, and as he explored he planted. He soon gained a legendary presence in frontier America. His solitary ways, rumors of his communion in nature, and his generous and devout Christian habits made him the perfect hero for the expanding nation. He died in Fort Wayne, Indiana, having planted more apple trees than could be counted all over the frontier.

When I was growing up about 45 miles south of Johnny Appleseed's final home in Indiana, we had an apple tree in my backyard right near my tree-house. I've wondered if the apples I ate off that tree were a winding but certain result of seeds that Johnny Appleseed planted in my home state.

We learn from the Johnny Appleseed way that just one fruitful life can leave behind a legendary influence. You ask the question "What will I be remembered for?" Only the seeds you plant in this life will be remembered in the next.

PLANTING SEEDS

The Master's Plan for multiplying fruit really does begin with…

How would you finish that sentence? Don't finish it by saying, "…people like me." That lets you off the hook a little bit. If it just begins with "people like you" then that's everyone. And if everyone's responsible usually no one takes responsibility. If Johnny Appleseed had simply planted one seed in his back yard and hoped everyone else was doing the same, he wouldn't have been remembered at all. His name would be more like Johnny Useless One-seed.

The key to living a life worth remembering is taking the responsibility yourself. Assume no one else is doing it—and act accordingly. Because that's closer to the reality than assuming everyone else is doing it. They're usually not.

The key to living a life worth remembering is taking the responsibility yourself.

Are you? That's the question. Finish that sentence now... The Master's Plan for multiplying fruit really does begin with …

_____

(Write "me" in your own handwriting in this blank)

The plan for multiplying fruit really does begin with me. Just one person, planting seeds!

"I am the vine; you are the branches. If you remain in me and I remain in you, you will bear much fruit; apart from me you can do nothing."—Jesus in John 15:5

Week Six
36.37.38.39.40.
Group Questions

1) Have each member of your group share how good he or she was in school when it came to math. What did you like about the subject? What didn't you like? What sort of teachers did you have?

2) Review: What are the four key fruit multipliers?
   i)

   ii)

   iii)

   iv)

3) How are you at multiplying disciples in your own family?

4)   Report to the group those people you are currently mentoring or have decided to in-vest in. Think of someone that is a non-Christian who you might be able to mentor or invest in.

5)   How is our group doing with the "Three Legged Stool" of community?

6)   How can our group be a part of multiplying churches?

7)   Share stories or dreams about real life fruit in the lives of people in the group.

Acknowledgements
Who made it possible...

God the Father created in me a dear love for the written word and the legacy it can leave. May all the glory go to God if anything I write becomes the fruit for which I am remembered.

God the Son loved me and gave himself for me (Galatians 2:20) and I owe him my salvation. May all the glory for each and every new disciple in the Kingdom go to him.

God the Holy Spirit often moved in my broken vessel as I wrote these words. Any inspired thought, idea or application is a credit to the Spirit. Any misstep remains a product of my own weakness.

My wife Kathy believes in me more than I believe in myself. And that is just one of the joys I have discovered in marriage. I thank her for pushing me and empowering me to just do it.

Spring Lake Wesleyan Church is my happy home in the west Michigan corner of the Kingdom. The church and its leaders gave me time to do this work, the immediate application in our 40 Days to see it lived out in community, and overwhelming high belief and trust in me along the way. She's the best church under the Son, and I'm honored to continue to serve her!

And to many more who made it possible...
- **Dad...** thanks for teaching me to write and developing me every year of my life.
- **Mom...** thanks for teaching me and all of us that it's never too late to take it to another level.
- **Jean Syswerda...** I can't thank you enough for your constructive help early and your gifted editing in the end.
- **Dennis Jackson & Pete Yoshonis...** thanks for taking a risk on me, pastoring me and for being my writing cheerleaders.
- **Zach Aument & Nate Mihalek...** for your creative work on the cover and interior layout, respectively.
- **Darcie Jackson...** thanks for ordering my ministry world and being faster than Fed Ex.
- **Anne Montgomery, Julie Kuyt & Mary Beth Witte...** for your detailed copy edit on the book.

- **SLWC Staff...** thanks for all the encouragement along the way, and for keeping me focused on the journey.
- **Steve Deur...** thanks for the accountability and the creativity.
- **Rob Paterson...** thanks for your tireless friendship and for walking through brokenness with me.
- **Max, Karina & Lauren...** thanks for reminding me daily about the fruit that matters most of all, which is my children.

NOTES

1. Unless otherwise noted all Scriptures used in *The Fruitful Life* are from the *New International Version* (NIV) Colorado Springs: International Bible Society (1978, 1984). Other versions cited include:

> NLT – *New Living translation*, Wheaton, IL: Tyndale House Publishers (1996)
> NRSV – *New Revised Standard Version*, Grand Rapids: Zondervan Publishing House (1990)
> KJV – *King James Version*
> WEV – *Worldwide English Version,* SOON Educational Publications

2. *The Message* Bible Paraphrase by Eugene Peterson

3. Found on pages 82-116 of *The Three Colors of Love* by Christian Schwarz (ChurchSmart Resources: ISBN 1-889638-45-5)

4. ibid. p82

5. The transliterated Hebrew word is "Shabar"

6. *Front Porch Tales* by Phillip Gulley. Sisters, Oregon: Multnomah Books. © 1997. pages 17-19

7. *ESPN The Magazine,* September 13, 2004 Issue

8. Archie and Peyton Manning with John Underwood. New York: Harper Entertainment. © 2000. page 281

9. I'm always intrigued by those books that say they are the "so-and-so's Bible." I mean books like the "Southern Gardener's Bible" or the "Computer Gamer's Bible" or even "The Tattoo Artist's Bible." In an age when the authority of the Bible is questioned by the academic world—the culture uses the very word "Bible" to mean "Authoritative Source of Everything." I think God laughs hard at this and in my strange mind I see him ordering boxes of these "bibles" from Amazon.com in his free time as practical joke gifts for parties in heaven.

10. The professors at a school I attended in Boston often would say, "There is no salvation without revelation." Revelation is God's way of communicating through multiple means. Creation is therefore a revelation. The inner light we have that draws us to wonder about God's existence is a revelation. The Bible is the written revelation of God. Jesus himself was a revelation of God in the flesh, and that's why Christ was called Immanuel, meaning "God with us." (Matthew 1:23)

11. Generational Church Attendance Statistics taken from 2004 numbers at The Barna Group, Ltd.

12. Relevant passages about these two churches are found in Acts 11:19-29; 13:1-3 & 15:1-41

Go to www.fruitful-life.com
for more on the
fruitful life journey.